6-18-63      H. C. Thiessen      24

# GREEK PAPYRI

## OF THE FIRST CENTURY

# GREEK PAPYRI
# OF THE FIRST CENTURY

*By*

W. HERSEY DAVIS

———

PRESENTED TO

ARCHIBALD THOMAS ROBERTSON

ON THE OCCASION OF

HIS SEVENTIETH BIRTHDAY

———

HARPER & BROTHERS PUBLISHERS

*NEW YORK AND LONDON*

1933

# PREFACE

THE purpose of this little book is to introduce students of Greek, especially of the Greek New Testament, to the Greek papyri of the first century with its linguistic and historical bearing on the literature of the Greek New Testament.

This small volume is presented to Dr. Archibald Thomas Robertson in honor of his seventieth birthday, November 6, 1933, and in recognition of his signal success in the field of the Greek New Testament. He now has closed his forty-fifth and has begun his forty-sixth year of continuous teaching in the Southern Baptist Theological Seminary. His pupil and friend and colleague now offers this volume to him as a small token of admiration and appreciation of his surpassing abilities and monumental work, of love for him, and of prayer that his life with its blessing presence may continue for many years to come.

For permission to make use of the documents I make grateful acknowledgment to the Trustees of the British Museum, the committee of the Egyptian Exploration Society, The John Rylands Library, the University of California, and the Curators of the Berlin Museums.

W. HERSEY DAVIS

*The Southern Baptist Theological Seminary*
*Louisville, Kentucky*

# TABLE OF CONTENTS

| | | | |
|---|---|---|---|
| BIBLIOGRAPHY | | | ix |
| INTRODUCTION | | | xix |
| TEXTS, TRANSLATIONS, AND NOTES: | | | |
| I. LETTER OF HILARION TO HIS WIFE ALIS | P.Oxy. 744 | B.C. 1 | 1 |
| II. ACCOUNT OF FOOD | P.Oxy. 738 | A.D. 1 | 8 |
| III. RECEIPT FOR HAY | P.Ryl. 183 | A.D. 16 | 10 |
| IV. RECEIPT FOR HAY | P.Ryl. 183(a) | A.D. 16 | 13 |
| V. LETTER OF RECOMMENDATION | P.Oxy. 292 | A.D. 25 | 16 |
| VI. LETTER OF RECOMMENDATION | P.Oxy. 787 | A.D. 16 | 21 |
| VII. LETTER TO HERACLIDES | P.Oxy. 2148 | A.D. 27 | 24 |
| VIII. PETITION TO THE CHIEF OF POLICE | P.Ryl. 130 | A.D. 31 | 28 |
| IX. LETTER OF HERMOGENES TO HARUOTES | P.Oxy. 1480 | A.D. 32 | 32 |
| X. PETITION TO THE STRATEGUS | P.Ryl. 135 | A.D. 34 | 36 |
| XI. LETTER OF A DAUGHTER TO HER MOTHER | P.Oxy. 295 | A.D. 35 | 40 |
| XII. LETTER TO PAUSANIAS FROM HIS TWO SONS | P.Oxy. 1672 | A.D. 37–41 | 43 |
| XIII. LETTER OF AMMONIUS TO APHRODISIUS | P.Ryl. 229 | A.D. 38 | 47 |
| XIV. CENSUS RETURN | P.Oxy. 255 | A.D. 48 | 52 |
| XV. LETTER OF MYSTARION TO STOTOETIS | B.G.U. 37 | A.D. 50 | 57 |

| | | | |
|---|---|---|---|
| XVI. NOTICE OF DEATH | P.Oxy. 292 | A.D. 61 | 60 |
| XVII. INVITATION FROM DIDYMUS TO APOLLONIUS | B.G.U. 596 | A.D. 84 | 63 |
| XVIII. LETTER FROM GEMELLUS TO SABINUS | P.Fay. 114 | A.D. 100 | 67 |
| XIX. LETTER OF HORUS TO APION | P.Oxy. 299 | 1st Cent. | 71 |
| XX. QUESTION TO THE ORACLE | P.Fay. 137 | 1st Cent. | 74 |
| XXI. LETTER OF THEON TO SARAPOUS | P.Oxy. 1154 | 1st Cent. | 76 |
| INDEX | | | 79 |

# BIBLIOGRAPHY

THIS brief Bibliography was selected for students who are beginning the study of the Greek papyri.

## COLLECTIONS OF PAPYRI

P.Amh.          The Amherst Papyri, ed. B. P. Grenfell and A. S. Hunt. 2 vols. London, 1900–01.

B.G.U.          Aegyptische Urkunden aus den Koeniglichen Museen zu Berlin: Griechische Urkunden: vols. I–IV; aus den Staatlichen Museen: Griechische Urkunden: Vols. V–VIII. Berlin, 1895–1933.

P.B.M.          Greek Papyri in the British Museum. Vols. I, II, ed. F. G. Kenyon; Vol. III, ed. F. G. Kenyon and H. I. Bell, Vols. IV, V, ed. H. I. Bell. London 1893–1917.

C.P.H.          Corpus Papyrorum Hermopolitanorum. Part I, ed. C. Wessely. Leipzig, 1905.

C.P.R.          Corpus Papyrorum Raineri. Vol. I, Griechische Texte, ed. C. Wessely. Vienna, 1895.

P.Cairo Preis.     Griechische Urkunden des Aegypt-
ischen Museums zu Kairo. Ed. F.
Preisigke. Strassburg, 1911.

P.Eleph.     Elephantine-Papyri. Ed. O. Ru-
bensohn. Berlin, 1907.

P.Fay.     Fayum Towns and their Papyri.
Edd. B. P. Grenfell, A. S. Hunt,
and D. G. Hogarth. London, 1900.

P.Flor.     Papiri Fiorentini. Vols. I–III. Edd.
G. Vitelli and D. Comparetti.
Milan, 1906–15.

P.Gen.     Les Papyrus de Genève I. Ed. J.
Nicole. Geneva, 1896–1900.

P.Giss.     Griechische Papyri zu Giessen I.
Edd. O. Eger, E. Kornemann, and
P. M. Meyer. Leipzig, 1910–12.

P.Goodsp. Cairo     Greek Papyri from the Cairo Museum. Ed. E. J. Goodspeed. Chi-
cago, 1902.

P.Grenf. I.     An Alexandrian Erotic Fragment,
and other Greek Papyri, chiefly
Ptolemaic. Ed. B. P. Grenfell.
Oxford, 1896.

P.Grenf. II.     New Classical Fragments, and
other Greek and Latin Papyri.
Edd. B. P. Grenfell and A. S.
Hunt. Oxford, 1897.

P.Hamb.        Griechische Papyrusurkunden der
               Hamburger Staats-und Universi-
               taetsbibliothek I. Ed. P. M. Meyer.
               Leipzig and Berlin, 1911–1924.

P.Hib.         The Hibeh Papyri, Vol. I. Edd.
               B. P. Grenfell and A. S. Hunt.
               London, 1906.

P.Iand.        Papyri Iandanae, Parts I–IV. Edd.
               E. Schaefer, L. Eisner, L. Spohr,
               and G. Spiess. Leipzig, 1912–14.

P.Leid.        Papyri Graeci Musei antiquarii
               publici Lugduni-Batavi, 2 vols.
               Ed. C. Leemans. 1843, 1885.

P.Lille        Papyrus Grecs de Lille I, ed. P.
               Jouguet. Paris, 1907–23; II, ed.
               J. Lesquier. Paris, 1912.

P.Lips.        Griechische Urkunden der Papy-
               russammlung zu Leipzig I. Ed. L.
               Mitteis. Leipzig, 1906.

P.Meyer        Griechische Texte aus Aegypten.
               Ed. P. M. Meyer. Berlin, 1916.

P.Oxy.         The Oxyrhynchus Papyri. Vols.
               I–VI. edd. B. P. Grenfell and
               A. S. Hunt; Vols. VII–IX. ed. A.
               S. Hunt; Vols. X–XV. edd. B. P.
               Grenfell and A. S. Hunt; Vol.
               XVI. edd. B. P. Grenfell, A. S.

Hunt, and H. I. Bell; Vol. XVII. ed. A. S. Hunt. London, 1898–1927.

P.Par.     Paris Papyri in Notices et Extraits XVIII. ii. Ed. Brunet de Presle. Paris, 1865.

P.Petr.     The Flinders Petrie Papyri in the Proceedings of the Royal Irish Academy—"Cunningham Memoirs," Nos. VIII., IX., and XI. Parts I. II. ed. J. P. Mahaffy; Part III. edd. J. P. Mahaffy and J. G. Smyly. Dublin, 1891–4.

P.Rein.     Papyrus Grecs et Demotiques. Ed. Th. Reinach. Paris, 1905.

P.Rev. L.     Revenue Laws of Ptolemy Philadelphus. Ed. B. P. Grenfell. Oxford, 1896.

P.Ryl.     Catalogue of the Greek Papyri in the John Rylands Library, Manchester; Vol. I., ed. A. S. Hunt; Vol. II. edd. J. de M. Johnson, V. Martin, and A. S. Hunt. Manchester, 1911–15.

P.S.I.     Papiri Greci e Latini della Societa Italiana I–IX, i., ed. Vitelli and others. Florence, 1912–1928.

P.Strass.   Griechische Papyrus zu Strass-
            burg I, II. Ed. F. Preisigke. Leip-
            zig, 1912–1920.
P.Tebt.     The Tebtunis Papyri. Vol. I. edd.
            B. P. Grenfell, A. S. Hunt, and
            J. G. Smyly; Vol. II. edd. B. P.
            Grenfell, A. S. Hunt, and E. J.
            Goodspeed. London, 1902–7.


## HANDBOOKS, GRAMMARS, LEXICONS, AND GENERAL REFERENCE WORKS

*(Only the books used or quoted are listed)*

Abbott-Smith, Manual Greek Lexicon of the New Testament, 2nd edit. Edinburgh, 1922.

Archiv, Archiv für Papyrusforschung. Ed. U. Wilcken. Leipzig, 1901–.

Blass-Debrunner, Grammatik des neutestamentlichen Griechisch. Sechste, durchgesehene und vermehrte Auflage. Goettingen, 1931.

Boisacq, Dictionnaire Etymologique de la Langue Grecque. Heidelberg and Paris, 1916.

Brugmann-Thumb, Griechische Grammatik. 4 Auflage. Munich, 1913.

Crönert, Memoria Graeca Herculanensis. Leipzig, 1903.

Dana, H. E., and Mantey, J. R., A Manual Grammar of the Greek New Testament. 1927.

Deissmann, Bible Studies. Edinburgh, 1901.

Deissmann, Light from the Ancient East. 4th edit. London, 1927.

Dieterich, K., Untersuchungen zur Geschichte der Sprache von der hellen. Zeit. Leipzig, 1898.

Dittenberger, Sylloge Inscriptionum Graecarum. 2nd edit.

Ebeling, H., Griechisch-deutsches Wörterbuch zum Neuen Testament. 1913.

Erman and Krebs, Aus den Papyrus der Königlichen Museen zn Berlin. Berlin, 1899.

Exler, F. X. J., The Form of the Ancient Greek Letter. A study in Greek Epistolography. Washington, D. C., 1923.

Gerhard, G. S., Untersuchungen zur Geschichte des griechischen Briefes. Dissertation. Tubingen, 1903.

Gildersleeve, B. L., and Miller, C. W. E., Syntax of Classical Greek. Part I, 1900. Part II, 1911.

Gradenwitz, O., Einführung in die Papyruskunde. Leipzig, 1900.

Grimm-Thayer, A. Greek-English Lexicon of the N. T. 1887.

Harsing, C. De optativi in chartis Aegyptiis usu. Bonn, 1910.

Hatzidakis, G. N., Einleitung in die neugriechische Grammatik. Leipzig, 1892.

Helbing, R., Auswahl aus griechischen Papyri. 2 Aufl. Berlin, 1924.

Helbing, R., Grammatik der Septuaginta: Laut-und Wortlehre. Gottingen, 1907.

Herwerden, H. van, Lexicon Graecum suppletorium et dialecticum. 2 vols. Leiden, 1910.

Hesychius, Hesychii Alexandrini Lexicon. Ed. M. Schmidt. Jena, 1867.

Horn, R. C., The Use of the Subjunctive and Optative Moods in the Non-literary Papyri. Philadelphia, 1926.

Hunt, A. S., and Edgar, C. C., Select Papyri with an English Translation. London, 1932.

Jannaris, A. N., A Historical Greek Grammar. London, 1897.

Kennedy, H. A. A., Sources of N. T. Greek. Edinburgh, 1895.

Kenyon, F. G., The Palaeography of Greek Papyri. Oxford, 1899.

Kühner-Gerth-Blass, Ausführliche Grammatik der griechischen Sprache. 2 Aufl. Hannover, 1890–1904.

Kuhring, G., De Praepositionum Graecarum in Chartis Aegyptiis Usu. Diss. Bonn. Bonn, 1906.

Laudien, A., Griechische Papyri. Weidmann, Berlin, 1912.

Lietzmann, H., Greek Papyri Selected and Explained. Cambridge, 1905.

Liddell and Scott, A Greek-English Lexicon. 8th Edition. Oxford, 1901. New (9th) Edition by H. S. Jones, Parts 1–7 (α to π), 1925–1933.

Mayser, E., Grammatik der Griechischen Papyri aus der Ptolemaerzeit:

Laut-und Wortlehre I. Leipzig, 1906.

Satzlehre II, 1 and 2. Berlin and Leipzig, 1926 and 1933.

Meecham, H. G., Light from Ancient Letters. London, 1923.

Milligan, G., Here and There Among the Papyri. London, 1923.

————Selections from the Greek Papyri.

New ed. Cambridge, 1927.

Milligan, G., New Testament and Its Transmission. London, 1932.

Mitteis and Wilcken, Grundzuge und Chrestomathie der Papyruskunde. Leipzig and Berlin, 1912.

Moeris, Moeridis Atticistae Lexicon Atticum. Ed. J. Pierson. Leiden, 1759.

Moulton, J. H., New Light from the Egyptian Rubbish Heaps. London, 1916.

Moulton, J. H., A Grammar of New Testament

Greek. Vol. I. Prolegomena. 3rd edit., 1908. Vol. II. Accidence and Word Formation. Finished by W. F. Howard, Edinburgh, 1929.

M.M., Moulton and Milligan, The Vocabulary of the Greek New Testament Illustrated from the Papyri and Other Non-literary Sources. 1914–1929. In one volume, 1930.

Moulton and Geden, A Concordance to the Greek New Testament. Edinburgh, 1899.

Olsson, Bror, Papyrusbriefe aus der frühesten Römerzeit. Uppsala, 1925.

Preisigke, F., Fachwörter des offentlichen Verwaltungsdienstes Aegyptens. Gottingen, 1915.

Preisigke, F., Wörterbuch der griechischen Papyrusurkunden mit Einschluss der griechischen Inschriften, etc. Band I and II, 1914–1927. Band III, Besondere Wörterliste, 1931. Vollendet von Emil Kiessling.

Radermacher, L., Neutestamentliche Grammatik. Das Griechische des N. T. in Zusammenhang mit der Volkssprache. 2 Aufl. Tübingen, 1925.

Robertson, A. T., A Grammar of the Greek New Testament in the Light of Historical Research. Fifth Edition, 1932.

Robertson, A. T., Word Pictures in the New Testament. 6 volumes (1930–1933).

Robertson-Davis, A New Short Grammar of the Greek Testament. New York, 1931.

Rossberg, C., De Praepositionum Graecarum in Chartis Aegyptiis Ptolemaeorum Aetatis Usu. Jena, 1909.

Schmid, W., Der Atticismus in seinen Hauptvertretern, etc. Stuttgart, 1887–97.

Schubart, W., Einführung in die Papyruskunde. Berlin, 1918.

Schubart, W., Ein Jahrtausend am Nil. 2 Aufl. Berlin, 1923.

Sophocles, E. A., Greek Lexicon of the Roman and Byzantine Periods. New York, 1887.

Souter, A., A Pocket Lexicon to the Greek New Testament. Oxford, 1916.

Suidas, Suidas Lexicon. Ed. I. Bekker. Berlin, 1854.

Thackeray, H. St. J., A Grammar of the O. T. in Greek. Vol. I. Accidence. Cambridge, 1909.

Thumb, A., Handbook of Modern Greek Vernacular. Translated from the German by S. Angus. Edinburgh, 1912.

Völker, F., Syntax der griechischen Papyri, I. Der Artikel. Munster, 1903.

Witkowski, S., Epistulae Privatae Graecae. 2 edit. Leipzig, 1911.

Ziemann, F., De epistularum Graecarum formulis sollemnibus quaestiones selectae. Halle, 1910.

# INTRODUCTION

THERE have been few discoveries in the field of archaeology in recent years that have attracted so much attention and have proved so valuable as the thousands of papyrus documents which have been unearthed from the rubbish-heaps and sands of Egypt. We are not here concerned with the Egyptian papyri written in the old Egyptian language (either hieroglyphic, or hieratic, or demotic), nor with the papyri written in Aramaic, or Latin, but with the papyri written in Greek and especially that of the Graeco-Roman and Roman periods. These Greek papyri contain our earliest copies of certain parts of the New Testament, portions of collections of non-canonical sayings of Jesus, portions of works of authors which were believed to be hopelessly lost to us, parts of texts of works (already known to us) of many classical authors, and thousands of private letters, official correspondence, wills, leases, memoranda, contracts, decrees, petitions, anything and everything.

## 1. *Papyrus as Writing Material.*

Both the art of writing and the use of papyrus as writing material in Egypt go back into an indefinite antiquity. Papyrus was in use certainly about 4000

B.C. (Kenyon, Palaeography, p. 14). A chief place
among the unknown immortals is due the genius
who first made use of the papyrus plant for writing.
It is difficult for us, to whom paper is cheap and
plentiful and to whom it sometimes seems a curse
and the making and reading of books a weariness to
the flesh, properly to appreciate the boon bequeathed
us by the mind that invented the papyrus sheet.
Chisel and stone, stylus and clay tablet were cum-
bersome and cramping, to say the least; with these
no real literature could be produced.

The method of preparation of the papyrus sheet
from the papyrus, *Cyperus papyrus* (L.), a kind of
sedge, which at one time grew in abundance in the
Nile valley but now is no longer to be found in
Egypt, was as follows: The outer covering of the
plant being stripped off, the pith of the stem consisting of pellicles of a papery nature was cut into
long thin strips which were laid down vertically on
a flat table to form the outer or lower layer. Over
this a second layer was laid across the first, at right
angles to it, so that the fibres now ran horizontally.
Then Nile water (where possible), because of its
muddy condition acting as glue, was used to moisten
the two layers which were pressed together to make
a single sheet. After being dried in the sun, it was

smoothed with a shell or bone. It was now ready for writing.

The size of the sheets varied considerably. A common size for non-literary documents was 5 to 5½ inches in width, and 9 to 11 inches in height. Larger sheets were made for important documents, attaining a height sometimes of 16 to 18 inches. When more space than a single sheet was needed, a number of sheets were joined together to form a roll of the required length. A common size for a papyrus-roll seems to be about 20 sheets (10 to 18 feet in length). It has been estimated that Mark's Gospel would occupy a roll of about 19 feet, while that for Luke's Gospel would be about 31 feet.

The side of the papyrus-sheet on which the layers ran horizontally was the smoother for writing, and is technically called the *recto*; the other side is called the *verso*, on which addresses, headings, and directions could be written. When fresh sheets were not available the *verso* was frequently used, even of old documents. Papyrus was by no means a cheap article. Sometimes the writing on the *recto* was washed out.

The writing tools of a scribe were reed brushes (the writing end bruised) or pens (the point cut, as with a quill-pen), ink (a mixture of lamp-black, water, and gum), and a palette of wood, ivory, slate or alabaster. The size of the palette varied in length from 8 to 16 inches, in width 2 to $3\frac{1}{2}$ inches.

## 2. *Discoveries.*

The earliest discoveries of which we have any knowledge of papyri in Egypt was in 1778 at Gizeh where some Arabs accidentally came upon some fifty rolls. When no purchasers could be found, all these except one roll (Charta Borgiana, in Museum at Naples), were destroyed. With the exception of some calcined rolls discovered at Herculaneum in 1752, the fact that papyri have been found only in Egypt is due to the dry climate.

No more discoveries were made until 1820 when some papyri were found around Memphis and Thebes. The documents were found enclosed in a single vessel, but for greater profit they were divided and sold separately; and so the collection is scattered among the principal museums of Europe.

In 1877 a great mass of papyri was unearthed at Crocodilopolis; but there was no method to the work of excavation, and probably a half of the material found by the native diggers perished altogether; the remainder went to Vienna to the collection of the Archduke Rainer.

In 1889 systematic exploration for papyri was undertaken by Professor Flinders Petrie at the site of a Ptolemaic cemetery at Gurob, a town near the mouth of the Fayum. From the mummy-cases many valuable papyri were secured.

The great period of papyri-discoveries on a scientific basis was ushered in by Drs. Grenfell and Hunt at Oxyrhynchus, the modern Behneseh, in 1896. From that time the work of exploration went steadily on at Oxyrhynchus until 1907. Drs. Grenfell and Hunt are probably the most expert discoverers and learned interpreters of the papyri.

The success of Drs. Grenfell and Hunt at Oxyrhynchus gave a great impetus to the work of papyrus-hunting. Soon German, French, and Italian expeditions were in the field and attained considerable success.

### 3. *Publications.*

The papyrus-documents so far discovered are in collections at all the great museums and libraries in Europe and America. The most important collections are at the British Museum, Queen's College (Oxford), the Louvre (Paris), Vienna Library, the Berlin Museum and the Cairo Museum.

Publications of these collections, made or being made, are named either from the locality where the documents were discovered or from the place where they are now kept, as the Oxyrhynchus Papyri, the

Hibeh Papyri, the Tebtunis Papyri, or British Museum Papyri, Chicago Papyri, John Rylands Papyri, the Berlin Papyri, the Amherst Papyri, etc. There are now about 10,000 published documents and as many more unpublished. Of these published texts 2156 texts have now been published in seventeen volumes of Oxyrhynchus Papyri (edited by Grenfell and Hunt). It is reported that it will take about the same number of additional volumes to complete the publication of the collection.

## 4. *Classification.*

The papyri are commonly classified under two general heads, literary and non-literary, with the Biblical and theological texts occupying an intermediate position (cf. Milligan, Here and There, p. 19).

About 1000 of the papyri now published are literary or classical texts, of which Homer claims about a third, other ancient writers already known to us less than a third, and more than a third is claimed by new writings, or writings of authors who had previously been only names in a classical dictionary. Among these last is the Persae of Timotheos (of Miletus), the oldest Greek literary manuscript in existence, dating from the fourth century B.C. Other new texts that may be specially mentioned are sev-

eral orations of Lysias; six speeches of Hyperides,
the contemporary and rival of Demosthenes; parts
of five plays (comedies) of Menander; a number of
fragments of the Hypsipyle of Euripides; a number of
Sappho's songs; a number of the Paeans of Pindar;
about 1300 lines of the Odes of Bacchylides, a contemporary of Pindar; the mimes of Herondas; the
lost work of Aristotle on the Constitution of Athens;
parts of the Hellenica, a piece of work by an unknown Greek historian of the first rank, which deals
with the history of Greece in the years 396 and 395
B.C.—this work has been variously assigned, to
Ephorus, Theopompus, or Cratippus.

Of all the discoveries of papyrus-documents certain Biblical and theological fragments aroused the
deepest and most widespread interest, such as the
Sayings of Jesus Christ. It is surprising that with
so many documents there are only about twenty-
five or thirty fragments of the LXX. And there now
have been published only thirty-five fragments of
the New Testament. "Notwithstanding this, six at
least are of outstanding interest, if only because they
belong to the third century, and are, therefore, from
a hundred to a hundred and fifty years, older than
the great Vellum MSS, such as the Codex Vaticanus
or the Codex Sinaiticus." Among the new documents
is the leaf of a papyrus-book which, at the time of

its discovery, was reckoned "to be a fragment of the oldest known MS of any part of the N. T." It begins with the opening words of the N. T., "The book of the generation of Jesus Christ" (Matt. 1:1). Dating about the fourth century is the largest find made as yet in N. T. texts, about one third of the Epistle to the Hebrews, copied out on the back of a roll, the *recto* of which contains the new Epitome of Livy. It includes the later chapters which are wanting in the Vatican Codex. Only mention can be made of part of a non-canonical gospel; the Logia of Jesus; liturgical works; a fragment of a Christian hymn of the third century which is "by far the most ancient piece of church music extant, and may be placed among the earliest written relics of Christianity"— additional interest attaches to it because it is accompanied by musical notation; a collection of prayers from the third century, one of which is headed "Prayer of the Apostles, Peter, and the rest"; a sixth century copy of the Nicene Creed; and letters and documents of the fourth century dealing with the church organization.

While the literary, Biblical and theological papyri are of supreme importance and interest to the scholar, yet not without interest for the general reader, the greatest human interest attaches to the non-literary papyri. The contents of these documents are as wide as life itself. We can here only indicate their significance for the most varied fields of human learning. Their value to the historian and the jurist is immediately patent; the geographer can reconstruct the map of ancient Egypt with precision; the palaeographer has an uninterrupted series of examples of ordinary script exactly dated from the third century B.C. to the eighth century A.D.; the philologist can now determine the nature and extent of the Koine (the common Greek of the period) and its relation to the dialects of the classical period; the student of the Greek N. T. can now see that the N. T. was written in the Koine of its period. Their value for the lexicographer and grammarian of the N. T. is worth all the labor that one may bestow upon them.

## 5. *Dating of the Papyri.*

The earliest dated Greek papyrus we possess is a marriage contract (P. Eleph. 1) of the year 311–10 B.C. From that time there is almost a continuous chain of documents extending well into the Byzantine period. Many of these documents are exactly dated by year and month and day. Official documents are generally so dated until the end of the first century A.D., and thereafter only by month and day. The formulas of dating differ, like the handwriting, in the Ptolemaic, Roman, and Byzantine periods. In a Ptolemaic document the date is given by the regnal year of the reigning sovereign, and the full formula will contain also a list of the priesthoods of all the defunct Ptolemies. The shorter formula is more general.

Roman dates are given by the regnal year of the emperor, but in a more business-like way. In Roman dates, as well as Ptolemaic, the year began with 1st Thoth (August 29). The first year of a sovereign lasted only from his accession to the 1st Thoth next ensuing.

At the time of the revolution under Diocletian this system of dating was abandoned, and dating by the consuls of the year was substituted. But in the year 312 A.D. the system of the indiction was instituted. This was a 15 year period, the origin of which is uncertain. The dating of Byzantine documents has given much trouble.

But many papyri are not exactly dated by the year, and month, and day. Yet with a high degree of certainty the century may fairly be determined by the style of handwriting, the contents of the document, and the circumstances in which the document is found. In some cases the year may safely be determined by comparison of its contents, style of writing, etc. with other dated documents. R.

## 6. *Table of Months.*

| Egyptian | Macedonian | Roman (Honorific) | In regular years corresponding to our |
|---|---|---|---|
| Θώθ | Δῖος | Σεβαστός / Γερμανικός | Aug. 29–Sept. 27 |
| Φαῶφι | 'Απελλαῖος | .................. | Sept. 28–Oct. 27 |
| 'Αθύρ | Αὐδναῖος | Νέος Σεβαστός / Δομιτιανός | Oct. 28–Nov. 26 |
| Χοιάκ | Περίτιος | Νερώνειος / Νερώνειος Σεβαστός / 'Αδριανός | Nov. 27–Dec. 26 |
| Τῦβι | Δύστρος | .................. | Dec. 27–Jan. 25 |
| Μεχείρ | Ξανδικός | .................. | Jan. 26–Feb. 24 |
| Φαμενώθ | 'Αρτεμίσιος | .................. | Feb. 25–Mar. 26 |
| Φαρμοῦθι | Δαίσιος | .................. | Mar. 27–Apr. 25 |
| Παχών | Πάνημος | Γερμανίκειος | Apr. 26–May 25 |
| Παῦνι | Λώιος | Σωτήριος | May 26–June 24 |
| 'Επείφ | Γορπιαῖος | .................. | June 25–July 24 |
| Μεσορή | Ὑπερβερεταῖος | Καισάρειος | July 25–Aug. 23 |
| αἱ ἐπαγόμεναι (ἡμέραι)...................... | | | Aug. 24–Aug. 28 |

The Egyptians for a long time reckoned time according to a solar year of 365 days, consisting of 12 months of 30 days each and 5 intercalary days (called ἐπαγόμεναι) which were added at the close of the year. But this year lacked about ¼ day of being equal to the true solar year. This was later corrected by adding an extra day every four years at the end of the year. Every four years, then, six ἐπαγόμεναι were added, and thus every four years Thoth 1 fell on Aug. 30. In such intercalary years (A.D. 3–4, 7–8, etc.) the English equivalents have to be advanced one day till our Feb. 29, after which the old correspondence is restored.

## 7. *Note on Method of Publication.*

The texts are given in modern printing with accentuation and punctuation. Square brackets [ ] indicate a lacuna in the original. Letters inserted within square brackets indicate the editors' proposed restoration. Letters in round brackets ( ) indicate the resolution of a symbol or abbreviation. Angular brackets ⟨ ⟩ are used to enclose letters, words, or phrases accidentally omitted in the original. Braces { } enclose superfluous letter or letters. Double square brackets ⟦ ⟧ enclose letters that have been erased in the original. Dots placed within brackets represent approximately the number of letters lost or deleted; dots outside brackets indicate mutilated or otherwise illegible letters. Letters with dots under them are to be considered doubtful.

Iota subscript does not occur in documents until about the 12th century A.D. Iota adscript has been printed where so written, otherwise iota subscript is employed.

# GREEK PAPYRI

## OF THE FIRST CENTURY

# I

## LETTER OF HILARION TO HIS WIFE ALIS

### B.C. 1

P.Oxy. IV, 744. Discovered and edited by Grenfell
and Hunt in *Oxyrhynchus Papyri*. Now in the Museum of Victoria University, Toronto, Canada. See
also Lietzmann, *Greek Papyri*, p. 8f.; Witkowski,
*Epist. Priv. Gr.*, p. 131f.; Helbing, *Auswahl aus Gr.
Pap.*, pp. 71–4; Deissmann, *Light*, pp. 167–70; Milligan, *Selections*, p. 32f.

'Ιλαρίων{α} "Αλιτι τῆι ἀδελφῆι πλεῖστα χαίρειν καὶ Βεροῦτι τῇ κυρίᾳ μου καὶ 'Απολλω-
νάριν. γίνωσκε ὡς ἔτι καὶ νῦν ἐν 'Αλεξανδρέᾳ ⟨ἐ⟩σμέν. μὴ ἀγωνιᾷς ἐὰν ὅλως εἰσ-
5 πορεύονται, ἐγὼ ἐν 'Αλεξανδρέᾳ μένω.
ἐρωτῶ σε καὶ παρακαλῶ σε ἐπιμελή-,
θ⟨ητ⟩ι τῷ παιδίῳ καὶ ἐὰν εὐθὺς ὀψώνιον λάβωμεν ἀποστελῶ σε ἄνω. ἐὰν
πολλαπολλῶν τέκῃς ἐὰν ἦν ἄρσε-
10 νον ἄφες, ἐὰν ἦν θήλεα ἔκβαλε.
εἴρηκας δὲ 'Αφροδισιᾶτι, ὅτι μή με
ἐπιλάθῃς. πῶς δύναμαί σε ἐπιλαθεῖν; ἐρωτῶ σε οὖν, ἵνα μὴ ἀγωνιάσῃς.
15 (ἔτους) κθ Καίσαρος Παῦνι κγ.

1

*On the verso*

'Ιλαρίων. "Αλιτι ἀπόδος.

"Hilarion to Alis his sister, many greetings, and to Berous my lady and to Apollonarin. Know that we are even now still in Alexandria. Keep from worrying, if all of them return, I remain in Alexandria. I beg you and beseech you, take care of the little child, and as soon as we receive wages I will send (them) up to you. If of all things you bear a child, if it is a male, let it alone (live); if it is a female, cast it out. You have told Aphrodisias, "Do not forget me." How can I forget you? I beg you therefore that you do not worry.

In the year 29 of Caesar, Pauni 23.

(Addressed)

Hilarion. Deliver to Alis."

1. "Αλιτι: For feminine proper names with stems in τ see Mayser, Band I, p. 273ff. ἀδελφῆι, "sister," from the tenor of the letter "wife" of Hilarion. It was a well established custom in Egypt to address one's wife as "sister" and one's husband as "brother." See Deissmann, *Light*, p. 168; Helbing, p. 72f.

τῆι ἀδελφῆι = τῇ ἀδελφῇ: The iota (ι) in the dative, locative, and instrumental cases was written on the line with the other letters—"adscript"; while with us (since the twelfth century) it is, except in the case of capital letters, written under the vowel—

"subscript." In the early papyri ι is found correctly written (adscript), and is never left off, because it was pronounced. Then later it ceased to be pronounced, and from about 200 B.C. it was frequently left off or it was placed where it did not belong (irrational iota). See Robertson, p. 194; Mayser, I. p. 119ff.

2. χαίρειν: This is common Greek formula of a greeting found at the beginning of letters. It is the absolute use of the infinitive: see Robertson, p. 1092. Cf. Acts 15:23; 23:26; Jas. 1:1; 2 John 10:11. Sometimes the imperative or the optative is used.

τῇ κυρίᾳ μου: a courteous mode of address. See 2 John 1, 5. In P.Oxy. 1679, 1, 3, 16 and P.Leip. 110, 1, 24 κυρία is applied to a mother. In P.Fay. 130, 1, 21 a brother is addressed with κύριε. Cf. P.Oxy. XII. 1481, 1; 1482, 1.

2–3. Ἀπολλωνάριν = Ἀπολλωναρίῳ: the short form (pet-name) is not declined.

4. ⟨ἐ⟩σμέν: σμεν was written in the papyrus, an instance of aphaeresis (infrequent in the papyri; see Mayser, I. p. 144).

μὴ ἀγωνιᾷς: a rare example at this date (1 B.C.) of the use of the present subjunctive in prohibitions, which is common in modern Greek. See Mayser, II. p. 147; Horn, p. 93, 101. Cf. Gildersleeve, Part I. p. 150; Brugmann-Thumb, *Gr. Gram.* p. 575; Jannaris, *Hist. Gr. Gram.* pp. 448f., 565f. (historically traced through examples); Hatzidakis, *Einleitung*, p. 226; Thumb, *Mod. Gr. Ver.* p. 127; Robertson, p. 853f.

ὅλως = in toto; we would expect ὅλοι instead of the adverb. Cf. B.U.G. III. 846, 9, σαπρῶς περιπατῶ, "I go around in dirty rags." See Robertson, p. 545; Blass-Debrunner, 434. Cf. P.Berol. 11662, 20 (Olsson, 34). But ὅλως may = πάντως.

6. ἐρωτῶ = "beg," "request," as frequently in the Koine. See Robertson, pp. 66, 80, 90. See Horn, p. 107f. It is frequently found both alone and in connection with παρακαλῶ; cf. 1 Thess. 4:1.

6–7. ἐπιμελήθ⟨ητ⟩ι in N. T. is found with the gen.; here with the dat., as in P.Tebt. I. 58, 62f.; for earlier instance see Kühner-Gerth, II. 1, 419. See Robertson, p. 509.

7. ἐὰν εὐθύς probably introduces a temporal clause, "as soon as"; see Horn, p. 134. If it is a conditional clause it is "if we soon receive," etc.

7–8. ὀψώνιον was originally used for an article of food; in the Koine period it frequently has the meaning of "money," "salary," soldier's "pay"; see the word in Preisigke, *Wörterbuch*, and in M.M., *Vocabulary*. In 2 Cor. 11:8 is found the same phrase which seems to be a regular formula. For "soldier's pay" see Luke 3:4; 1 Cor. 9:7. See Robertson, pp.

65, 66, 80, 155; Deissmann, *Light*, p. 168; Meecham, *Light*, p. 68.

8. σε = σοι. There was a growing tendency in the vernacular for the accusative to take over the functions of the dative. For the N. T. see Robertson, pp. 467, 535. Cf. Jannaris, *Hist. Gr. Gr.* p. 341f; Hatzidakis, *Einleitung*, p. 221ff; Meecham, *Light*, p. 77.

9. πολλαπολλῶν or πολλὰ πολλῶν: The meaning of this phrase is not yet clear. "Good luck," "May God protect," "May God avert," "May the gods cause to turn out well," "altogether too much," and "too much," are some of the meanings that have been suggested.

9–10. ἐὰν ἦν: ἦν here is subjunctive = ᾖ. Horn, pp. 27–30, clearly shows that ἦν is used as a subjunctive form; see the many examples cited by him. See Robertson, p. 220; Moulton, *Proleg.*, p. 168; Vol. II. pp. 113, 204. For the addition of an irrational ν see Mayser, Band I, pp. 191–194; Jannaris, *Hist. Gr. Gram.*, pp. 100 547f

ἄρσενον = "male," a vernacular formation on ἄρσην. Cf. P.B.M. III. 909a, 5 (136 A.D.), κάμηλον ἄρσενον; B.G.U. 88, 6 (147 A.D.), κάμηλον ἄρρενον. WH. have ἄρσην and not ἄρρην; for the spelling and use of these words see Robertson, 217f; Moulton, II. p. 103f.

10. θήλεα = θήλεια: ε is often found for ει, especially before α; see Mayser, I. 67f; Cronert, *Mem. Gr. Herc.*, p. 111, N5; Robertson, p. 187; Moulton, II. p. 81f. In line 4 'Αλεξανδρέᾳ = 'Αλεξανδρείᾳ.

ἔκβαλε: Justin Apol. I. 27ff. condemns the heathen custom of exposing children. Deissmann (*Light*, p. 169) quotes from LXX, Exod. 1:16 (cf. 22): ἐὰν μὲν ἄρσεν ᾖ, ἀποκτείνατε αὐτό. ἐὰν δὲ θῆλυ, περιποιεῖσθε αὐτό. Cf. Gal. 4:30; Luke 7:19. See Angus, *Environment*, p. 48f.

11. εἴρηκας: for this use of the perfect (the vernacular historical perfect) see Robertson, pp. 898–902.

'Αφροδισιᾶτι: the messenger who brought the reminder to Hilarion.

ὅτι frequently is used to introduce direct quotation; for this "recitative" ὅτι see Robertson, p. 1027f. με (and σε in l. 12): the accusative in the Koine period began to displace other cases which generally followed certain verbs; ἐπιλανθάνομαι was generally followed by the genitive, rarely by the accusative (see Phil. 3:13). Cf. Hatzidakis, *Einleitung*, p. 220ff; Jannaris, *Hist. Gr. Gr.*, p. 334. See Robertson, pp. 472f, 509. For μὴ and the aorist subjunctive in prohibitions see Robertson, pp. 851–854.

12. ἐπιλάθῃς: second aorist active subjunctive.

12–13. ἐπιλαθεῖν: the second aorist active forms of this verb are rare; the active form ἐπιλανθάνω, as of

other verbs which regularly occurred in the middle,
began to be used in the vernacular in place of the
middle; see Hatzidakis, *Einleitung*, p. 197ff, Mayser,
II. p. 116.

13. ἐρωτῶ ἵνα μὴ ἀγωνιάσῃς: For this sub-final use of
ἵνα in object clauses after verbs of striving, beseech-
ing, etc., see Robertson, pp. 991–994; cf. 1 Thess.
4:1; cf. Schmid, *Atticismus*, III. p. 80f.

15. Καίσαρος: When the name Καῖσαρ occurs alone
in the date of a papyrus it generally means Augustus.

*Verso.* ἀπόδος: "deliver," aorist act. imperative; in
an early form of address it is found very frequently
in the papyri; see Ziemann, p. 278f.

## ACCOUNT OF FOOD

### A.D. 1

P. Oxy. IV. 738. Discovered and edited by Grenfell and Hunt in Oxyrhynchus Papyri. Now in the Library of Graz University, Austria.

. . . . . . .

δίπνωι ε .

Κανωπικὸν

ἧπαρ.

δίπνῳ ζ .

5  ὄστρεα ι,

θρίδαξ α.

δίπνωι ζ .

ἀρτίδια β,

ὄρνις σιδυτὴ ἐξ ὕδα(τος) α,

10  πτέρυγες β.

. . . . . .

"For dinner on the 5th, a Canopic liver; for dinner on the 6th, 10 oysters, 1 lettuce; for dinner on the 7th, 2 small loaves, 1 fattened bird from the water, 2 snipe (?)."

1. δίπνωι = δείπνῳ: For ι = ει see No. III, 11; for iota adscript see No. I, 1. This papyrus is a fragment

of a list of articles of food consumed on different days.

2. Κανωπικόν: adjective of Κάνωπος or Κάνωβος, an island-town in Lower Egypt, on the western mouth of the Nile; it was notorious for its luxury; the adjective is used also of a district around the western mouth of the Nile.

6. θρίδαξ is the usual spelling of this word. In P. Oxy, 1212, 5 θρύδαξ occurs. Cf. Hesych. θιδρακίνη: θίδραξ καὶ θρίδαξ.

8. ἀρτίδια: For the frequency of diminutives see Robertson, p. 82.

9. σιδυτή = σιτευτή: "fattened." Cf. Herodianus, *Philetaerus*, p. 473: σιτευτοὺς ὄρνιθας, οὓς νῦν σιτιστοὺς λέγουσι. In Luke 15:23, 27, 30 is found the form σιτευτός, in Matthew 22:4 the form σιτιστός.

10. πτέρυγες: The editors (G. and H.) give the meaning "snipe." It is possible that the word means a vegetable.

# III

## RECEIPT FOR HAY

### A.D. 16

P. Ryl. II. 183. From the Arsinoite nome.

Ἀγχορίνφις Ἡρακλείδου προστάτης ἰδίων ὄνων
Ἀπολλωνίου τοῦ Ἀλεξάνδρο(υ) ἐπισπουδαστοῦ Ἀφροδ(ισίῳ)
καὶ Πετερμουθίωνι τοῖ(ς) δυσὶ Ἀσκληπ(ιάδου) χα(ίρειν). ἀπέχω
παρ᾽ ὑμῶν τὰς ἐπεσταλμένας μοι δοθῆναι
5 διὰ χρηματισμοῦ Εὐημέρου καὶ Φιλοξένου γενή(ματος)
πρώτου ἔτους Τιβερίου Καίσαρος Σεβαστοῦ
χόρτου διμνώου δέσμας χιλίας ἐν Εὐημερί[ᾳ
ἐν μηνὶ Μεσορὴ τοῦ β(ἔτους). / χό(ρτου) δέ(σμαι) ᾽Α. (ἔτους)
    β Τιβερίου
Καίσαρος Σεβαστοῦ Μεσορὴ ιγ.
10 ἔγραψεν ὑπὲρ αὐτοῦ Μάρων γρ(αμματεὺς) κτηνοτρόφω(ν)
    Εὐη(μερίας)
διὰ τὸ μὴ ἰδέναι αὐτὸν γράμματα.

"Anchorimphis son of Heraclides, superintendent
of the private donkeys of Apollonius son of Alexander,
transport-master, to Aphrodisius and Petermouthion,
the two sons of Asclepiades, greeting. I have received
from you the thousand bundles of . . . hay from
the produce of the first year of Tiberius Caesar
Augustus ordered to be delivered to me through the

10

notification of Euhemerus and Philoxenus in Euhemeria in the month Mesore of the 2nd year. Total
1,000 bundles of hay. The 2nd year of Tiberius
Caesar Augustus, Mesore 13.

Maron, secretary of the herdsmen of Euhemeria,
wrote for him because he does not know letters."

1. προστάτης: "superintendent"; cf. the fem. προστάτις (Rom. 16:2), "protectress," "patroness," a development from the political sense of προστάτης
(patron).

ἰδίων: "private" as opposed to public or imperial.
See Robertson, p. 691f.

2. ἐπισπουδαστοῦ: an official whose duty was to
superintend the transport of the state corn-dues, to
see that the transportation was made expeditiously.

3. τοῖς δυσί: the normal dative form in the Koine;
cf. Mayser, I. p. 314. See No. IV. 1, 3. For the form
and use in N. T. see Robertson, pp. 251, 282, 76f.

χαίρειν: see No. I, 1–2.

ἀπέχω = "I have received"; it is a technical expression regularly used in writing a receipt. For this
aoristic present with the "perfective" force of the
preposition see Robertson, pp. 577, 828, 866. Cf.
Matt. 6:2, 16ff.; Luke 6:24; Phil. 4:18; see Deissmann, *Light*, p. 110f.; cf. Mayser, I. p. 487, II.
pp. 133f., 167.

5. γενήματος, "produce," is used of vegetable prod-

ucts, from γίνομαι; γέννημα (from γεννάω) is used of animal products, as "offspring," "child." See Mayser, I. p. 214; Blass-Debrunner, p. 9; M.M., p. 123; Robertson, p. 213.

7. διμνώου: the meaning is not known; it seems to have to do either with the weight or with the grade of hay. See P. Soc. 400, 12.

8. The sign / = γίνονται, used in giving the total number; a technical term used in stating a total.

Μεσορή: the name of the Egyptian month is indeclinable.

10. ἔγραψεν . . . γράμματα: the phrase occurs in hundreds of papyrus-documents which were written in whole or in part by a scribe (or other person) for a person who does not know how to write.

ἔγραψεν: for the "epistolary aorist" see Robertson, p. 846f.

ὑπέρ: "for," "instead of"; for ὑπέρ and the ablative with resultant meaning of "instead of" see Robertson, p. 630ff.

11. ἰδέναι = εἰδέναι; for ι = ει see Mayser, I. pp. 87–94; Robertson, p. 195ff.

γράμματα = characters formed in writing, letters of the alphabet; see Gal. 6:11.

# IV

## RECEIPT FOR HAY

### A.D. 16

P.Ryl. II. 183 (a). From the Arsinoite nome.

Πτολεμαῖος Λεωνίδου προστάτης
ὀνηλασίου ὄνων Ἀπολλωνίου τοῦ Ἀλεξάνδ(ρου)
Ἀφροδισίωι καὶ Πετερμουθίωνι ἀμφοτέροις
Ἀσκληπιάδο(υ) χα(ίρειν). ἀπέχω παρ' ὑμῶν ἀπὸ λόγου
5 ἀγορασμοῦ χόρτου γενή(ματος) β (ἔτους) Τιβερίου
Καίσαρος Σεβαστοῦ χόρτ[ο]υ διμνώου
δέσμας χιλίας, / χόρτ(ου) δέ(σμαι) Ἀ. ἔγραψεν
ὑπὲρ αὐτοῦ Μάρων γρ(αμματεὺς) αὐτοῦ διὰ
τὸ βραδύτερ[ο]ν̣ [αὐ]τὸν γράφιν.
10 (ἔτους) γ Τιβερίου Καίσαρος Σεβαστοῦ, μη(νὸς) Σεβαστοῦ
ε.

(2nd hand) Πτολεμαῖος ἀπέχω.

"Ptolemaeus son of Leonides, superintendent of
the driving-stable of asses of Apollonius son of Alexander, to Aphrodisius and Petermouthion, both sons
of Asclepiades, greeting. I have received from you on
account of the purchase of hay of the harvest of the
2nd year of Tiberius Caesar Augustus a thousand
bundles of . . . hay. Total 1,000 bundles of hay.
Maron his secretary wrote for him because he writes

13

very slowly. The 3d year of Tiberius Caesar Augustus, the 5th of the month Sebastus.

I Ptolemaeus have received."

1. προστάτης: See No. III. 1.

3. Ἀφροδισίωι ( = — ῳ) with iota adscript. In the papyri ι is not written under a vowel (subscript) but on the line with the vowel (adscript). Iota was not written subscript until the twelfth century A.D. See Robertson, p. 194.

ἀμφοτέροις: "both" (two); see No. III. 3. where τοῖς δυσί is used of the same brothers. See Robertson, pp. 251f., 744f.; Blass-Debrunner, pp. 38, 151f.

4. χαίρειν: See No. III. 3.

ἀπέχω: See No. III. 3.

λόγου: For λόγος in the sense of "account," "reckoning," see Preisigke, *Wörterbuch*, s. v.; M.M. *Voc.* s. v. See Deissmann, *Light*, p. 117. Cf. Phil. 4:15, 17. Cf. P.Oxy. III. 525, 8–9, ἐκ τοῦ ἐμοῦ λόγου, "at my expense."

5. γενήματος: See No. III. 5.

7. For the sign / see No. III. 8.

ἔγραψεν ὑπὲρ αὐτοῦ: See No. III. 10.

9. βραδύτερον: "very slowly"; for the "elative" comparative of the adverb see Robertson, p. 665; cf. Blass-Debrunner, p. 139. In the phrase "to write slowly" each of the adverbs βραδέως, βραδύτερον,

βραδύτερα, or βραδέα is found. Paul the Apostle may have used an amanuensis because he wrote slowly.

γράφιν = γράφειν: See No. III. 11; for itacism see Mayser I, pp. 63–130; Robertson, pp. 187–198.

10. μηνὸς Σεβαστοῦ: "Sebastus," the honorific Roman name of the Egyptian month Θώθ.

12. Πτολεμαῖος ἀπέχω: thus Ptolemaeus appends his own signature written in rude uncials to authenticate the whole document. Cf. Paul's reference to his authenticating signature in 2 Thess. 3:17, 18; cf. Gal. 6:11. See Milligan, *Here and There*, p. 40f.

# V

## LETTER OF RECOMMENDATION

### A.D. 25

P.Oxy. II. 292. Discovered at Oxyrhynchus and edited by Grenfell and Hunt. Now in the University Library, Cambridge. See also Lietzmann, *Greek Papyri*, p. 7; Milligan, *Greek Papyri*, No. 14; Laudien, *Griech. Papyri*, No. 9; Olsson, *Papyrusbriefe*, p. 68ff.

Θέων Τυράννωι τῶι τιμιωτάτωι
πλεῖστα χαίρειν.
Ἡρακλείδης ὁ ἀποδιδούς σοι τὴν
ἐπιστολήν ἐστίν μου ἀδελφός·
5 διὸ παρακαλῶ σε μετὰ πάσης δυνάμεως ἔχειν αὐτὸν συνεσταμένον. ἠρώτησα δὲ καὶ Ἑρμί[α]ν
τὸν ἀδελφὸν διὰ γραπτοῦ ἀνηγεῖ[σθαί
σοι περὶ τούτου. χαρίεσαι δέ μοι τὰ μέγιστα
10 ἐάν σου τῆς ἐπισημασίας τύχηι.
πρὸ δὲ πάντων ὑγια⟨ί⟩νειν σε εὔχ[ο-
μαι ἀβασκάντως τὰ ἄριστα
πράττων.          ἔρρω(σο).
*On the verso*
          Τυράννωι διοικ(ητῇ).

"Theon to his most esteemed Tyrannus, many

16

greetings. Heraclides, the bearer of the letter to you, is my brother. Therefore I entreat you with all (my) power to hold him as one recommended (to you). I requested also Hermias your brother by letter to communicate with you concerning this. You will show me the greatest kindness if he (Heraclides) gain your notice. Above all things I pray that you may without harm from the evil eye be in good health and faring prosperously. Good-bye.

(Addressed)

To Tyrannus, dioecetes."

1. τῶι τιμιωτάτωι: For iota adscript see No. I. 1; for the superlative form and the meaning see Robertson, p. 670; cf. Acts 23:26.

2. χαίρειν: See No. I. 2.

3. ὁ ἀποδιδούς is a regular phrase for "the bearer" of a letter. The form ὁ ἀποδιδῶν occurs in B.G.U. VIII. 1871, 3 (57–6 B.C.); the participle of ἀναδίδωμι in the same sense is found in B.G.U. 775, 9; P.Fay. 130, 15; P.Oxy. 532, 11, etc.; and of the simple form of δίδωμι in P.Oxy. 937, 30.

5. παρακαλῶ: See No. I. 6.

μετὰ πάσης δυνάμεως. For μετὰ with the genitive to denote accompaniment (manner) see Robertson, p. 611f.

6. ἔχειν αὐτὸν συνεσταμένον. In the papyri συνίστημι (recommend, commend) is found frequently in letters

of recommendation. The practice of sending "letters
of commendation" was common. For the word and
for reference to the practice in the N. T. see Acts
9:2; 22:5; 1 Cor. 16:3; 2 Cor. 3:1. Cf. Rom. 16:1.
In P.Oxy. 1587 the phrase συστατικῶν γραμμάτων occurs, probably with a slightly different meaning
from συστατικῶν ἐπιστολῶν in 2 Cor. 3:1. For the construction and form of the phrase see Luke 14:18f.
where a similar construction is found (ἔχε με παρῃτη-
μένον); see Robertson, pp. 109, 1122. Some scholars
consider the phrase in Luke 14:18f. a Latinism (habe
me excusatum); see H. McLachlan, *St. Luke, The
Man and His Work*, p. 49.

7. ἠρώτησα: "I requested"; see No. I, 6. See Deissmann, *Bible Studies*, pp. 195, 200.

8. διὰ γραπτοῦ: "by letter," "in writing," as dis-
tinguished from "by word of mouth." Cf. P.Oxy.
293, 5–6, οὔτε διὰ γραπτοῦ οὔτε διὰ σημείον, "neither by
letter nor by message"; P.Oxy. 1061, 19 (22 B.C.)
διὰ γραπτοῦ ἠρώτησα.

9. χαρίεσαι (from χαρίζομαι) = χαριεῖ (the form of
the Attic future). In P. Grenf. II. 14 (c), 7 (264 or
227 B.C.) χαριεῖσαι occurs. This form, as well as
πίεσαι, φάγεσαι (Luke 17:8), καυχᾶσαι (1 Cor. 4:7),
and ὀδυνᾶσαι (Luke 16:25), is a fresh formation by
analogy with -σαι in the perfect middle (passive)
that corresponds to -μαι and -ται. Of course these

forms were condemned by the atticists: see Moeris, p. 16, ἀκροᾷ, Ἀττικῶς. ἀκροᾶσαι, Ἑλληνικῶς. For discussion of these forms in N. T. and Koine see Robertson, pp. 340, 355f.; Mayser, I. p. 328; Moulton, *Proleg.*, p. 53f., and II. p. 198; Jannaris, p. 197; Blass-Debrunner, p. 50. For LXX see Thackerary, *Gram*, p. 218.

10. ἐπισημασίας: "notice," "sign of approval."

11. πρὸ δὲ πάντων ὑγιαίνειν σε εὔχομαι: This phrase generally comes at the beginning of a letter. Cf. Ziemann, pp. 318, 333, 1; but see P.Oxy. 294, 30. Its occurrence at the end of a letter illustrates Jas. 5:12.

12. ἀβασκάντως ("without harm from the evil eye"), adverb from ἀβάσκαντος "not bewitched by the evil eye," "free from harm," a frequent expression for averting evil in closing greetings; see P.Oxy. 300, 9; 930, 23; P.Fay. 126, 10. See Gal. 3:1 for the verb from which ἀβασκάντως comes. See Robertson, p. 473; Meecham, p. 144f.; Deissmann, *Light*, p. 193, n. 10.

12–13. τὰ ἄριστα πράττων: "faring prosperously"; ἄριστα is elative superlative, as probably μέγιστα in line 9. See Robertson, pp. 278f., 670. πράττων has here been taken as anacoluthon for πράττοντα. There is a strong probability that it refers to the writer and is in agreement with the subject of εὔχομαι; in

which case the writer is saying that he himself is quite well. Cf. the old expression at the beginning of a letter, εἰ ἔρρωσαι, εὖ ἂν ἔχοι· καὶ αὐτὸς δ' ὑγίαινον. See Ziemann, p. 305ff.

13. ἔρρωσο (perf. pass. imperative) or ἔρρωσθε is the usual way of closing a letter, corresponding to the Latin *vale*, *valete*, farewell. Additions of terms of endearment etc. are frequently found, especially in the second and third centuries A.D. See Exler, *Epistol.*, p. 74ff.; Ziemann, pp. 335ff.

14. διοικητῇ: a financial officer in the χώρα. See Preisigke, *Fachwörter.*, s. v.

# VI

## LETTER OF RECOMMENDATION

### A.D. 16

P.Oxy. IV, 787. Discovered at Oxyrhynchus and edited by Grenfell and Hunt. The original is now in the Library of Columbia University, New York. See Olsson, *Papyrusbriefe*, p. 63f.

(The beginning of the letter is lacking. Five lines are given; but the editors did not divide the lines according to the papyrus.)

. . . ὡς ἔστιν ἡμέτερος. ἐρωτῶ σε οὖν ἔχειν αὐτὸν συνεσταμένον καὶ ἐν οἷς ἐάν σοι προσέρχηται [[ποι]] ἐκ δικαίου
εἰς τὴν ἐ[μ]ὴν καταλογὴν ποιήσεις αὐτῶι. [σ]ὺ δὲ ὑπὲρ ὧν
ἐὰν αἱρῇ γράφε.

". . . as he is our (friend or brother). I beg you therefore to hold him as one recommended (to you) and in whatever he approaches you justly you shall on my recommendation do for him. But you yourself, concerning whatever you choose, write (me)."

1. ὡς ἔστιν ἡμέτερος: almost certainly the last words of the introduction; cf. No. V, 4. In the N. T. ἡμέτερος is infrequent, as in the papyri; see Robertson, p. 685.

ἐρωτῶ = "I beg"; see No. I, 6; followed by the infinitive, see No. IV, 7; cf. Horn, p. 107f.

1–2. ἔχειν αὐτὸν συνεσταμένον: See No. V, 6.

2. ἐν οἷς ἐὰν σοι προσέρχηται: For the relative clause see Robertson, pp. 955–959; Mayser, I. pp. 261ff.; Blass-Debrunner, p. 209f.; ἐάν = ἄν, see Robertson, pp. 181, 190; Mayser, I. p. 152f.

προσέρχηται: This verb is used sometimes to mean "to approach (one) with a request." See Hebrews 11:6; 10:1; cf. Dio Cassius 56. g. τοῖς θεοῖς προσερχώμεθα. In this sense it is used frequently in the LXX.

⟦ποι⟧: The writer started to write ποιήσεις of line 3 in this place.

ἐκ δικαίου = "justly," reasonably; cf. the classical ἐκ τοῦ δικαίου. Cf. P.Oxy. IV, 746, 8.

3. εἰς τὴν ἐμὴν καταλογήν: "on my recommenda-tion," or "out of regard for me." Cf. P. Strass., II. 117, 4–5 εἰς τὴν καὶ Βάσσου καταλογήν; P.Oxy. IV. 811 ὅτι πάντα μοι ποιεῖ εἰς τὴν σὴν καταλογήν. For the mean-ing of εἰς with the acc. (= on the basis of) see Robert-son-Davis, p. 256. The possessive pronoun ἐμήν may be objective, and the phrase may be translated "out of regard for me"; for objective use of the poss. pron. see Robertson, p. 685. For the meaning and use of καταλογή see Van Herwerden, Lexicon, s. v.; Olsson, p. 54.

ποιήσεις: The volitive future is practically an imperative in sense; see Robertson, pp. 874, 942; Blass-Debrunner, p. 200; Mayser, I. p. 212.

αὐτῶι (= αὐτῷ): for ι adscript see No. I, 1.

3–4. σὺ δὲ ὑπὲρ ὧν ἐὰν αἱρῇ γράφε: cf. P.Oxy. VII. 1061. 20–21 καὶ σὺ δὲ γράφε ὑπὲρ ὧν ἐὰν θέλῃς. For ἐάν = ἄν, and for the relative clause with ἐάν, see note on line 3. For ὑπέρ ("concerning") sometimes in the sense of περί see Robertson, p. 632; cf. P. Lips. 104.13 περὶ ὧν αἱρῆσθε γράφετέ μοι (B.C. 96–5). Note the present imperative ("write from time to time") and the present subjunctive (αἱρῇ). For αἱρεῖσθαι in the sense of "wish" see Hesychius: αἱρήσασθαι · λαβεῖν, βουληθῆναι; and αἱροῦμαι · ——, ἢ λαμβάνω, ἢ βούλομαι.

# VII

## LETTER TO HERACLIDES

### A.D. 27

P.Oxy. XVII. 2148. Discovered by Grenfell and
Hunt, and edited by Dr. Hunt in Oxyrhynchus
Papyri.

. . . . . . . .

σι̣[ο
νομι̣[ . . . . ]πατ̣ . [ . ] . . .
ἐκομισάμην τὴν σε-
μίδ[αλ]ιν χρηστὴν οὖσαν.
5 παράβαλε εἰς οἶκον μή
τιν[ος] χρείαν ἔχῃ μή-
τηρ μου. ἀσπάζου Παυσειρίω(να)
καὶ Ἑρμίαν καὶ Ἡ[ρακλ]είδη(ν)
καὶ [ . . ] . ασταν καὶ [τὰς τ]ῶν
10 ἀδελφῶν σου γυναῖκας
καὶ τὰ τέκνα καὶ τοὺς
φιλοῦντός σε πάντας.
ἐὰν δέ σοι ἐμπέσῃ ὀψαρί-
διν σιναπηρόν, ἀγόρασον
15 καὶ ταρίχευσον ἡμεῖν.
ἐάν τι ποιῇς χρηστόν,
περιποίησον εἰς οἶκον

24

ἀδελ[φ]ῶν. τὰ δ'ἄλλα ἔρρωσ(ο).

(ἔτους) ιγ Τιβερίου Καίσαρος Σε-
20    βαστοῦ,

Ἐπεὶφ ιβ.

*On the verso*

εἰς Ὀξ[υ(ρυγχίτην)] Ἡρακλείδηι ἀδελφ[ῶι

" . . . I received the fine flour which was good.
Run over to the house lest my mother has need of
anything. Give my regards to Pausirion and Hermias
and Heraclides and . . . and your brothers' wives and
the children and all those who love you. If you come
upon any mustard relish, buy it and make pickle for
us. If you are making anything good, make some extra for the brothers' house. And for the rest, good-bye.
The 13th year of Tiberius Caesar Augustus, Epeiph
12. (Address on verso)

To the Oxyrhynchite (nome), for brother Heraclides."

3. ἐκομισάμην: "I received." The middle of this
verb occurs frequently in the papyri with the meaning of "receive," e.g. P. Fay. 114, 3–4 (100 A.D.)
κομισάμενός μου τὴν ἐπιστολήν, "having received my
letter," "on receipt of my letter." The middle in the
N. T. seems in all its occurrences to have the meaning
"receive back," "recover," with which it is also
found in the papyri, e.g. P.Tebt. I. 45. 33 (113 B.C.)

ἵνα . . . ἐγὼ μὲν κομίσωμαι τὰ ἐμαυτοῦ, "in order that I may recover my property."

5. παράβαλε: in the sense of "go," "betake oneself," "run over to"; see B.G.U. III. 824. 14 (55–6 A.D.) παράβαλε οὖν ἐκεῖ (for ἐκεῖ with verb of motion see Robertson, p. 548, and cf. Rom. 15:24). Cf. Acts 20:15.

5–6. μή . . . ἔχῃ: For this infrequent construction in a final clause see Robertson, p. 987f.

7. ἀσπάζου: This word is used in the common formula for conveying greetings at the end of a letter. See Ziemann, p. 326ff. For the three general forms of greeting see J. Arm. Robinson, *Comm. on Eph.*, p. 280. It is frequent in the N. T.

11–12. τοὺς φιλοῦντάς σε πάντας: See Titus 3:15; and cf. P.Fay. 118.25 (110 A.D.) ἀσπάζου τοὺς φιλοῦντές σε πάντες πρὸς ἀλήθιαν, "salute all who love you truly."

13–14. ὀψαρίδιν (= ὀψαρίδιον) is a double diminutive. For increase in the use of diminutives in the Koine and the N. T. see Robertson, pp. 82, 155; Jannaris, pp. 291–294. For the growing practice of shortening the endings of diminutives (-ιον > -ιν) see Jannaris, pp. 113f., 291ff.; Mayser, pp. 154, 260. Cf. the form ὀψάριον in John 6:9, etc.

14. σιναπηρόν is a new adjective, "with mustard."

15. ἡμεῖν = ἡμῖν; for ει = ι see Mayser, pp. 87–94; Robertson, p. 195f.

16. χρηστόν: "good;" for its use in reference to things cf. P. Cairo Zen. III. 59349.7 (244 B.C.) εἰ ἔστιν ἤδη χρηστόν, "if it (wine) is now fit for use"; also Luke 5:39. See line 4.

18. ἀδελφῶν is probably not to be taken literally, but as members of a society; see Robertson, p. 80f.; Deissmann, *Light*, pp. 98, 107.

τὰ δ'ἄλλα: Accusative of general reference used adverbially; see Robertson, pp. 486f., 294.

# VIII

## PETITION TO THE CHIEF OF POLICE

### A.D. 31

P.Ryl. II. 130. From Euhemeria (Arsinoite nome).
Edited by Johnson, Martin and Hunt.

'Αθενοδώρωι ἐπιστάτῃ φυλακειτῶν
παρὰ Πρωτάρχου τοῦ Πτολεμαίου.
νυκτὶ τῇ φερούσῃ εἰς τὴν δ
τοῦ ἐνεστῶτο(ς) μηνὸς Φαῶφ(ι)
5 τοῦ ιη (ἔτους) Τιβερίου Καίσαρος Σεβαστοῦ
ἐπιβαλόντες τινὲς λῃστρικῶι
τρόπῳ εἰς τὸν ὑπάρχοντά μοι
περὶ Εὐημερείαν τῆς Θεμίστο(υ)
μερίδος ἐλαιῶνα ἐν τῇ γωνίᾳ
10 ἐτρύγησαν ἐκ τῶν καρπῶν
οὐκ ὀλίγην ἐλᾶν, ἔτι δὲ καὶ
πλεῖστάκι ὡσαύτως ἐτρύ-
γησαν καὶ ἀπηνέγκαντο.
διὸ ἀξιῶι, ἐὰν φαίνηται, συν-
15 τάξαι γράψαι ἀναζητῆσαι
ὑπὲρ τοῦ μέρους πρὸς τὴν ἐσομένην ἐπέξοδον.
εὐτύχ(ει).

"To Athenodorus, chief of police, from Protarchus

son of Ptolemaeus. On the night leading to the 4th of the present month Phaophi of the 18th year of Tiberius Caesar Augustus, certain persons making a thievish attack on the olive-orchard that belongs to me in the vicinity of Euhemeria of the division of Themistes at the corner, gathered of the fruits a quantity of olives; and furthermore they repeatedly gathered (them) in the same way and carried (them) off. Wherefore I request (you), if it seems good (to you), to give orders to write that investigation be made concerning the matter with a view to the ensuing punishment. Farewell."

1. Ἀθενοδώρωι: for ι adscript see No. I. 1.

ἐπιστάτῃ: "chief," used here in its original sense of "overseer." See Luke 5:5; 17:13 where it seems to = Rabbi.

φυλακειτῶν = φυλακιτῶν: "police," "guards;" for ει = ι see No. VII. 15.

3. νυκτὶ τῇ φερούσῃ εἰς τὴν δ: "on the night leading to the 4th" = "on the night before the 4th." The day began at sunrise. Cf. P.Tebt. I. 54. 8 (86 B.C.) τῆι νυκτὶ τῆι φερούσηι εἰς τὴν κε τοῦ Φαῶφι. See Smyly, Hermathena, XI. pp. 87ff. Cf. τῇ ἐπιφωσκούσῃ εἰς μίαν σαββάτων, Matt. 28:1. For φέρω εἰς = "lead to" see Acts 12:10; and cf. P.Oxy. I. 69. 1 (190 A.D.). For the frequency of the locative without preposition in expressions of time see Robertson, p. 522f.

6. ἐπιβαλόντες: intransitive use of ἐπιβάλλω, "make an attack;" see Jannaris, p. 357; Robertson, pp. 80, 797f. Cf. P.Tebt. II. 52, 4.

6–7. λῃστρικῶι τρόπῳ: "in the manner of thieves (or robbers)," a common phrase in complaints of theft.

8. περὶ Εὐημερείαν: cf. Acts 28:7 περὶ τὸν τόπον ἐκεῖνον, "in the neighborhood of that place."

8–9. τῆς Θεμίστου μερίδος: "of the division of Themistes," a district of the Arsinoite nome. μερίς occurs often in the papyri and regularly for a geographical division. Cf. Ramsay, *Exp.* V. vi. p. 320.

9. ἐλαιῶνα: "olive-orchard." Cf. Acts 1:12. The existence of this New Testament word had been questioned; but the number of its occurrences in the papyri is large. See Robertson, p. 154; Blass-Debrunner, p. 87; Deissmann, *Light*, p. 171, note 6.

11. οὐκ ὀλίγην: "not a few" = a quantity. ὀλίγος in this figure (litotes) is frequently found in the papyri. Cf. Luke 14:28.

12. πλειστάκι: a rare form, superlative adverb used in elative sense. Note the group of five adverbs in lines 11–12.

13. In these complaints of violence there is frequently added, after the account of the acts of violence and before the request, the sentence: βλάβος δέ μοι ἐπηκολούθησεν οὐκ ὀλίγον, "and no small damage

resulted to me," "I suffered no slight loss." See line
11 and cf. Luke's phrase οὐκ ὀλίγον.

14. ἀξιῶι (irrational iota): "I ask," "I request," a
general quasi-legal term in petitions addressed to
magistrates. It is generally followed by an infinitive as here. In petitions made to a king δέομαι is
generally used.

14. ἐὰν φαίνηται: "if it seems good (to you)," "if you
approve." This phrase (generally with σοι after ἐάν)
occurs very frequently in appeals, petitions, and the
like. See Horn, p. 38f. Cf. its use in Mk. 14:64
and Luke 24:11. Note the order of three infinitives.

16. ὑπὲρ τοῦ μέρους: for ὑπέρ used in the sense of
περί see Robertson, p. 632; see No. VI. 6. In the
papyri μέρος frequently has the meaning "matter";
cf. 2 Cor. 3:10; 9:3.

16–17. ἐσομένην. See Robertson, p. 877f. for this
use of the future participle.

18. εὐτύχει: a regular closing formula; see Ziemann,
p. 334f.

# IX

# LETTER OF HERMOGENES TO HARUOTES

A.D. 32

P.Oxy. XII. 1480. Discovered and edited by Grenfell
and Hunt; now in the Library of Trinity College,
Dublin. See Olsson, p. 74f.

Ἑρμογένης Ἀρυώτῃ
τῷ προφήτῃ καὶ φιλ-
τάτῳ πλῖστα χαί(ρειν)
καὶ διὰ παντὸς ὑγιέ(νειν).
5 οὐκ ἠμέλησα περὶ
οὗ μοι ἐπιτέταχας.
ἐπορεύθην πρὸς
Ἑρμογένην τὸν κω-
μογρ[α]μματέαν, καὶ
10 ὁμολόγησέ μοι ποῆσε
τὴν ἀναβολήν. πεπόη-
τε εἰς τὸν ἐκλογιστήν.
λυπὸν ἠὰν δύνῃ ἐ[π]ισ-
τολὴν λαβῖν παρ' αὐ-
15 τοῦ τοῦ ἐκλογισ[τοῦ
ὡς Ἑρμογένει, ἵν[α
μὴ σχῇ τ[ . . . ] . . [ . . ,
παρακαλῶ [σε με-

γάλως π[έμψαι
20 τῷ υἱῷ μ[ου φά-
σιν μοι λ[ . . . . . .
περὶ αὐ[τοῦ . . . ,
καὶ γράψ[ον μοι περὶ
ὧν ἡ[ὰ]ν δύν[ω-
25 με κα[ὶ] ἠδή[ ως
ποήσω. ἔρρω[σο.
(ἔτους) ιη Τιβερίου Καίσαρος
Σεβαστοῦ Μεχ(εὶρ) ιθ.

*On the verso*

[ἀπόδ(ος) Ἁ]ρυώτῃ προφήτῃ παρὰ Ἑρμογ(ένους) Ἡρακ(λ ).

"Hermogenes to Haruotes the prophet, and dearest friend, many greetings and continual good-health. I did not neglect (the matter) about which you have given me instructions. I went to Hermogenes the comogrammateus, and he promised me to make the delay. He has arranged (the matter) with the eclogistes. Now then, if you are able to get a letter from the eclogistes himself for Hermogenes, that he may not get . . . , I beseech you greatly to send word to my son for me . . . , and write me concerning whatever I may be able (to do) and I will gladly do it. Good-bye.

The 18th year of Tiberius Caesar Augustus, Mecheir 19.

(Addressed on verso)

Deliver to Haruotes the prophet from Hermogenes son of Heracl (   )."

2. προφήτῃ: "prophet," a title of certain priests in Egypt.

3. πλῖστα = πλεῖστα: for ι = ει see No. III. 11.

4. ὑγιένειν = ὑγιαίνειν: for ε = αι see Mayser, p. 107; Robertson, p. 186.

5–6. περὶ οὗ κτλ: For the relative clause see Robertson, p. 720f.; cf. Rossberg, p. 42.

8. Ἑρμογένην: On the ν in the sing. acc. of proper names in the 3rd declension see Robertson, p. 258; Moulton-Howard, II. p. 139.

8–9. κωμογραμματέαν: "village-scribe." For ν in the acc. sing. of consonant stems see Robertson, p. 258f.; Moulton-Howard, II. p. 129f.

10. ὁμολόγησε = ὡμολόγησε: For augment see Robertson, p. 367f.; Mayser, p. 336; cf. Moulton-Howard, II. p. 190.

10–11. ποῆσε (= ποιῆσαι) τὴν ἀναβολὴν: "to make the delay"; but ἀναβολὴν in the papyri generally means "embankment," which it may have here; cf. P. Goodsp; Cairo, 15. 9, τὴν ἀναβολὴν πεποίημαι, "I have made the embankment." But cf. Acts 25:17. For the loss of ι from οι before vowels see Mayser, p. 108f. For ε = αι see line 4 above.

11–12. πεπόητε (=πεποίηται) εἰς τὸν ἐκλογιστήν.

Here it seems that ποιέω is used as πράσσω. But the editors translate: "He has made it as far as the eclogistes is concerned." The eclogistes was an Alexandrian official who examined the revenue-accounts of a nome—an auditor of the accounts of a nome.

13. λυπόν = λοιπόν: "now then"; used to mark a transition as οὖν is frequently used. See M.M. *Voc.*, s.v.; Sophocles, s.v.

ἠάν = ἐάν, see Mayser, p. 77.

14. λαβῖν = λαβεῖν: For ι = ει see line 3 above.

16. ὡς Ἑρμογένει: "for Hermogenes." Cf. a similar construction with ὥστε, P.Tebt. II. 280, 3 (126 B.C.) Ἡρακλείδει τραπεζίτῃ ὥστε βασιλεῖ, "to Heraclides the banker for the king."

20–21. φάσιν: "word," "information by report"; cf. P.Oxy., II. 293, 4, 8; IV. 805; Acts 21:31. Cf. Hesychius: φάσεις · —— , λόγοι, φῆμαι.

23–25. περὶ ὧν ἠὰν (= ἐὰν) δύνωμε (= δύνωμαι). For ἐάν (= modal ἄν) in relative sentences see Robertson, pp. 80, 181, 190f., 957f. For ε = αι see l. 4 above.

25–26. ἡδήως ποήσω = ἡδέως ποιήσω. For η = ε see Mayser, p. 62f.; for loss of ι in οι see ll. 10–11 above.

# X

## PETITION TO THE STRATEGUS

### A.D. 34

P.Ryl. II. 135. From Euhemeria (Arsinoite nome).
Edited by Johnson, Martin and Hunt.

Λυσανίᾳ στρατηγῶι Ἀρσινοείτου
παρὰ Ἀρτεμιδώρου τοῦ
Ἰραναίου. τῇ νυκτὶ φερούσηι
εἰς τὴν κβ τοῦ Φαρμοῦθι τοῦ
5 ἐνεστῶτος κ (ἔτους) Τιβερίου Καίσαρος
Σεβαστοῦ ἐπιβαλόντος τινὸς
λιστρικῷ τρόπο εἰς ἃς γεωργῶ περεὶ Εὐημερίαν τῆς Θεμίστου μερίτος Μάρκου Ἀπολ⟨λω⟩νίου
10 Σατυρνίρου χόρτου ἦραν
διὰ ὄνον χόρτου δύσμας
τριάκοαν ἀπὸ ἀρουρῶν δύο.
διὸ δίδυμε τὸ ὑπόμνημα
ὕπος ἀναζητήσῃ ὁ τῆς
15 κώμης ἀρχήφοδος
καὶ ἀκθῆναι τοὺς αἰ-
δίους ἐπὶ σὲ ἔκξοδο(ν).

εὐτύχ(ει).

"To Lysanias, strategus of the Arsinoite nome,

from Artemidorus son of Irenaeus. On the night leading to the 22nd of Pharmouthi of the present 20th
year of Tiberius Caesar Augustus certain persons
making a thievish incursion into (the land) which I
cultivate belonging to Marcus Apollonius Saturn-
inus in the vicinity of Euhemeria in the division of
Themistes, carried off by donkeys thirty bundles of
hay from two arurae. Wherefore I present the peti-
tion in order that the archephodus of the village
may make an inquiry and the culprits be brought
before you for (fitting) punishment. Farewell."

1. στρατηγόι = στρατηγῷ: the chief officer of a district. For οι = ωι = ῳ see Mayser, pp. 132–7; Robertson, p. 200.

3–7. τῇ νυκτὶ κτλ. See No. VIII, 3–6 for comments.

3. φερούσηι: ι adscript see No. I, 1.

5. ἐνεστότος = ἐνεστῶτος, see Mayser, pp. 132–7;
Robertson, p. 200.

6. ἐπιβαλόντος τινός = ἐπιβαλόντες τινές: for ο in place
of ε see Mayser, p. 96; Robertson, p. 189. Cf. P.Tebt.
II. 52, 4 (114 B.C.) ἐπιβαλόντος (= ἐπιβαλόντες).

7. λιστρικὸ τρόπο = λῃστρικῷ τρόπῳ: For ο = ῳ see
Mayser, p. 137; Robertson, p. 200. For ι = η = ῃ
see Mayser, p. 82ff.; Robertson, p. 191.

εἰς ἅς: Generally a word like ἀρούρας (antecedent
of ἅς) is found in a position following Σατυρνίρου in

line 10. Cf. P.Ryl. II. 126, 16 εἰς ἃ . . . . . . . . . . . . . . .
ἐδάφη; see Robertson, p. 719ff.

7–8. γεοργῶ = γεωργῶ: for ο = ω see line 5 above.

8. περεί = περί: ει = ι, see Mayser, pp. 87–94; Robertson, p. 195ff.

9. μερίτος = μερίδος: τ for δ, see Mayser, p. 176f.

10. Σατυρνίρου = Σατυρνίλου = Σατυρνίνου: for ρ for λ and λ for ν see Mayser, pp. 186–8.

11. ὄνον = ὄνων: ο for ω, see line 5 above.

δύσμας = δέσμας: υ for ε is a peculiar vowel-change; cf. P. Fay. 119, 4, 5 (100 A.D.) δύσμην, and P. Tebt. II. 572 (2nd cent. A.D.) μωνοδυσμίας (= μονοδεσμίας).

12. τριάκοαν = a contraction of τριάκοντα with an irrational ν (see Mayser, pp. 197–9; Robertson, p. 220, Moulton, pp. 168, 187; Jannaris, p. 543f.).

13. δίδυμε = δίδωμι. The word generally used in this phrase is ἐπιδίδωμι. υ for ω is a rare peculiarity of vowel-change. Concerning ε for ι see Mayser, p. 80f. But δίδυμε may = δίδομαι.

13–17. See No. VIII, 14–17.

14. ὕπος = ὅπως: υ for ο, see Mayser, p. 97; cf. P. Oxy, II. 269, 9 (57 A.D.) δὺς (= δὸς) αὐτῷ ἀποχήν. ο for ω see line 5. For ὅπως with subjunctive and an infinitive as expressing the immediate purpose and the ultimate purpose see Robertson, p. 986f.

15. ἀρχήφοδος = ἀρχέφοδος; η for ε, see Mayser, p. 62f. An archephodus was a chief inspector of police.

16. ἀκθῆναι = ἀχθῆναι; κ before θ, see Mayser, p. 172.

16–17. αἰδίους = αἰτίους; δ for τ, see Mayser, p. 175f.

17. ἔκξοδον = ἔξοδον: The word generally used here in petitions is ἐπέξοδον and is customarily preceded by πρὸς τὴν δέουσαν (or τρὸς τὴν ἐσομένην) which the writer seems to have carelessly left out. Cf. Exler, p. 120f. See No. VIII, 16–17.

18. εὐτύχει: a regular closing formula; see No. VIII, 18; cf. Exler, p. 69, etc.

# XI

# LETTER OF A DAUGHTER TO HER MOTHER

## ABOUT A.D. 35

P.Oxy. II. 295. Discovered and edited by Grenfell
and Hunt. Now in the Library of Columbia University, New York. Olsson, *Papyrusbriefe*, p. 75.

Θαεισοῦς Συρᾶτι τῇ
μητρί. γίνωσκε ὅτι
Σέλευκος ἐλθὼν
ὧδε πέφευγε.
5 μὴ σκ{λ}ύλλε ἑα-
τὴν ἐνπῆναι.
προσδέχου ἱς τὸν
ἐνιαυτόν. Λου-
κία γράψον μοι
10 τὴν ἡμέραν.
ἄσπασαι σὺ
'Αμμωνᾶν
τὸ[ν] ἀδελφόν μου
κα[ὶ] .ραπ[.]ν καὶ
15 [τ]ὴ[ν ἀδε]λφὴν
[. . . . . .] α [. . .

*In the left hand margin*
καὶ Θεωνᾶν τὸν πατ[έ]ρα

"Thaisous to her mother Syras. Know that Seleu-
cus came here and has fled. Don't trouble yourself
to start (for home). Wait until the end of the year.
Lucia, write me the day. Salute Ammonas my brother
and . . . and my sister . . . and my father The-
onas."

1–2. Θαεισοῦς Συρᾶτι τῇ μητρί: Rarely before the
end of the third century A.D. is χαίρειν absent from
the opening formula of this kind; cf. Ziemann, p.
284. Exler (p. 64) has found only about a dozen of
this kind (without χαίρειν) in the period from the
third century B.C. to the third century A.D.

2. γίνωσκε ὅτι: for γινώσκω followed by ὅτι see P.Par.
47, 14 (153 B.C.); cf. 2 Tim. 3:1; followed by ὡς,
see No. I, 3. γίνωσκε (or γινώσκειν σε θέλω) is used very
frequently after the opening greeting. Cf. P.Oxy.
III. 528; IV. 743; etc.

4. ὧδε: this adverb is common after verbs of motion; it expresses both "hither" and "here"; see
Robertson, pp. 299, 548; Blass-Debrunner, p. 62.

5–6. μὴ σκύλλε ἐατήν (= ἑαυτήν): here ἑαυτήν =
σεαυτήν; ἑαυτοῦ, -ῆς, is often in the Koine found for
the first or second person; see Mayser, pp. 114f.,
303f.; Robertson, pp. 185, 287f. Cf. Luke 7:6, μὴ
σκύλλου; Mark 5:35; P.Oxy. XIV. 1669, 13 καὶ
σκύληθι (third century A.D.)—the passive has taken

over function of middle—"take pains" (to come here).

6. ἐνπῆναι = ἐμβῆναι or ἐμφῆναι. ἐμφῆναι does not suit so well as ἐμβῆναι. The editors translate the former by "to explain."

7. ἰς = εἰς: itacism, ι for ει, see Mayser, p. 87f.; Robertson, p. 195f.

8–9. Λουκία, γράψον: as a parallel construction the editors cite P.Oxy. II. 398, 22–3.

# XII

## LETTER TO PAUSANIAS FROM HIS TWO SONS

### 37–41 A.D.

P.Oxy. XIV. 1672. Discovered and edited by Grenfell and Hunt. Olsson, *Papyrusbriefe*, p. 76f.

Δημήτριος καὶ Παυσανίας Παυσαν[ί]αι
τῶι πατρὶ πλεῖστα χαίρειν καὶ ὑγι(αίνειν).
ᾗ ἡμέρᾳ ἐξέστης ἡμῶν πεπράκα-
μεν χό(ας) λβ ξένοις προσώποις ἐν οἷς
5  ἦν καὶ πολλὰ λέα οἰνάρια ⟦ὥστε⟧ ἐκ (δραχμῶν) ε μετὰ
χάριτος, ὥστε αἱ πράσεις ἡμῶν καλλιότεραι γε-
γ[ό]νασι λείαν, καὶ ἐλπίζομεν ὅτι
καλλιότεραι τούτων γενήσονται.
[δ]ι[ὸ γ]ράφομέν σοι ἵν' εἰδῇς πό-
10  τερόν σε δεῖ ἀνενέγκαι τὸ ὅλον
[ἢ] μέρος εἰς τὴν πόλιν. καλῶς
δὲ ποιήσεις ἐάσεις ἐν Πέλα
⟦[. .] . ρ . .⟧, ἵνα πραθῇ ⟦. . . . τὰ τῆς
[τ]ετάρτης ληνοῦ μόνης. ἐπιγνοὺς
15  [οὖ]ν τὸν παρὰ σοὶ ἀέρα ἱκανὸς ἔσῃ
περὶ πάντων. Μουνάτιος δὲ
ὁ φίλος συντυχὼν ἔλεγεν συμ-
[πε]φωνηκέναι τοῖς ἐκ τῆς κώ-

43

[μ]ης αὐτοῦ μετὰ χάριτος τοῖς ὅ-
20 [νοις] ἐκ (δραχμῶν) λβ. ἔρρω(σο).

*Second hand*

[(ἔτους). Γ]αίου ⟦Τιβερίου⟧ Καίσαρος Αὐτοκράτορος Σεβα-
  [σ]τοῦ

　　　　[Παῦ]νι κ[.

"Demetrius and Pausanias to Pausanias their father very many greetings and good health. On the
day on which you left us we sold thankfully to
(some) strange persons 32 choes (of wine) among
which there were also many small quantities of fine
wine at the rate of 5 drachmae, so that our sales
have become very much more favorable and we hope
that they will become more favorable than these.
We are therefore writing to you that you may know
whether it is necessary for you to carry up the whole
or a part to the city. You will do well to leave in
Pela to be sold the (wine) of the fourth vat only.
Then, having learned how the wind is with you, you
will be able (to decide) about all (the things).
Munatius, our friend, in a chance-meeting said that
he thankfully had agreed with the people of his
village about the donkeys (for transport) at the
rate of 32 drachmae. Good-bye.

The year . . . of Gaius Caesar Imperator Augustus, Pauni 2[ ]."

1–2. For this type of the opening phrase (with ὑγιαίνειν added) see Exler, p. 32f.

3. ᾗ ἡμέρᾳ κτλ: "on the day on which," etc.; see Robertson, pp. 522, 718f. For πεπράκαμεν see Robertson, p. 900.

4. προσώποις: "persons"; πρόσωπον is found in the Koine in the sense of "person."

5. λέα (= λεῖα): "fine." λεῖος is found with the meaning "excellent" (of its kind).

οἰνάρια: "small quantities of wine" seems to be the meaning here; see Olsson, p. 78f.

ἐκ δραχμῶν: "at the rate of 5 drachmae;" for ἐκ with the ablative to denote price, see Robertson, p. 599.

5–6. μετὰ χάριτος: "thankfully," almost = μετὰ χαρᾶς, "with joy"; see Olsson, p. 78. See line 19.

6. καλλιότεραι. For occurrences of the double comparative form in the N. T. and elsewhere, see Robertson, pp. 277f., 663f.; Blass-Debrunner, p. 37; Jannaris, p. 147; Mayser, p. 301; Moulton-Howard, II. p. 166.

7. λείαν (= λίαν, ει for ι see No. X, 8) is not frequently found with the comparative.

11–12. καλῶς ποιήσεις ἐάσεις. The same form occurs in P.Oxy, II. 297, 3 καλῶς ποιήσεις γράψεις. Commonly καλῶς ποιήσεις introduces a command or request. It is generally followed by an aorist participle of coincident action; but occasionally it is followed by an infinitive or an indicative (the future indicative in this place).

12. Πέλα: a town in the Oxyrhynchite nome.

14–15. ἐπιγνοὺς οὖν τὸν παρὰ σοὶ ἀέρα. The editors say: "It is rather tempting to take ἀέρα here in a metaphorical sense, like Latin *ventus* in e.g. Cic. *Clu.* 28.77 *rumorem et contionum ventos collegere*; but the writer may merely be referring to the suitability of the wind for river transport."

16. Μουνάτιος is the Greek spelling of the Latin name Munatius. He is evidently a wine-merchant.

19–20. τοῖς ὄ[νοις] (suggestion of Schmidt accepted by Olsson, p. 79, for the editors' τοῖς ο̣[. . .]). Thirty-two drachmae is the uniform rent for a donkey for transport.

# XIII

## LETTER OF AMMONIUS TO APHRODISIUS

A.D. 38

P.Ryl. II. 229. Edited by Johnson, Martin and Hunt.
See also Olsson, *Papyrusbriefe*, p. 80.

'Αμμώνιος 'Αφροδισίωι τῶι
    φιλτάτωι χαίρειν.
ἔγραψω ἐπιστολὴν πρὸς Ἡράκλη(ον)
τὸν π[ρ]οβατοκτη(νοτρόφον) ἵνα δοῖ σοι ὄνον,
5  καὶ Ὠφελίωνι ἐνετειλάμην
ἵνα καὶ αὐτὸς δοῖ ἑτέραν καὶ τοὺς
ἄρτους μοι πέμψηι. ἐπεὶ οὖν
ἔπεμψάς μοι (ἀρτάβας) γ ἐρωτῶ σε
ἐκ παντὸς τρόπου εὐθέως μοι
10  πέ[μ]ψαι τὰς ἄλλας (ἀρτάβας) γ καὶ τὸ
ὀψάριον, ἐπεὶ ἐν πλοίῳ εἰμί.
περὶ δὲ τῆς τροφῆς τῶν χοιριδίω(ν)
καὶ τοῦ λοιπ(οῦ) τῆς τιμῆ(ς) τοῦ χόρτου πρόχρησον ἕως οὗ παραγένωμαι·
15  δοκῶ γάρ, συναιρόμενος πρὸς σὲ
λογάριον παρεδεξάμην σοι πάντα.
παρακάλεσον οὖν τὴν γυναῖκά
σου τοῖς ἐμοῖς λόγοις ἵνα ἐπιμέληται τῶν χοιριδίων· ἐπιμέλου δὲ

20　καὶ τοῦ μόσχου.  πάντω(ς) δὲ, 'Αφροδίσιε,
　　τοὺς ἄρτους μοι πέμψον καὶ τὸ ὀψάριον.
　　ἐὰν δὲ θέλῃς γράψον μοι τίνι
　　δῶ εἰς τὸν χόρτο(ν) καὶ εἰς τροφὴ(ν) ἄλλας (δραχμὰς) κ.
　　ἔρρω(σο). (ἔτους) β Γαίου Καίσαρος Σεβαστοῦ Γερμανικο(ῦ)
25　　Μεχ(εὶρ) κζ.

*On the verso*

　'Αφροδισίωι ἐπιστάτῃ.

"Ammonius to his dearest Aphrodisius greeting.
I wrote a letter to Heracleus the herdsman that he
should give you a donkey, and I gave orders to
Ophelion that he himself also should give (you)
another (donkey) and send me the loaves. Now since
you just sent me 3 artabae (of bread), I beg you by
all means to send me immediately the other 3 artabae
(of bread) and the fish, as I am on board a boat. As
to the pigs' food and the rest of the price of the hay
advance payment until I come; for, I think, as I was
settling accounts with you I gave you allowance for
everything. Now urge your wife from me that she
take care of the pigs; but you take care of the calf.
By all means, Aphrodisius, send me the loaves and
the fish. And if you will, write me to whom I shall
give a further 20 drachmae for the hay and food.
Good-bye.

The 2nd year of Gaius Caesar Augustus Germanicus, Mecheir 26.

(Addressed) To Aphrodisius, agent."

1–2. The phrase of this type of opening formula came into use when the Roman republic changed into an empire. Its occurrence in this letter is one of the earliest examples. See Exler, p. 62f.

1. τῶι = τῷ: For ι adscript see No. I, 1.

3–4. ἔγραψα . . . ἵνα δοῖ: For this sub-final use of ἵνα, as also with ἐνετειλάμην in line 5, see Robertson, pp. 992ff., 1046; Blass-Debrunner, p. 218f.; Moulton, *Proleg.*, p. 208; Radermacher, pp. 190ff.

δοῖ: This form (in l. 6 also) of the subjunctive is much commoner than it was at first supposed. It is probably due to Ionic influence. See Robertson, p. 308f.; Mayser, p. 325; Horn, p. 26; Moulton-Howard, II. pp. 83, 204, 210.

6. ἑτέραν (sc. ὄνον), "another donkey," "a second donkey"; see Robertson, p. 748.

7. οὖν: "now . . . just"; for the use of οὖν in transition see Robertson, p. 1191.

9. ἐκ παντὸς τρόπου: "by all means," like the ordinary παντὶ τρόπῳ. Cf. κατὰ πάντα τρόπον, Rom. 3:2; and Phil. 1:18.

8 and 10. ἀρτάβας γ (sc. ἄρτων). Loaves of bread were generally measured in artabae, and the number was given in pairs of loaves. See Olsson, p. 81.

11. ὀψάριον here almost certainly means "fish"; cf. John 21:10.

13–14. πρόχρησον: "advance payment"; this word

(aor. imper.) is not from προχρῄζω, but from προκίχρημι or προκιχράω; see Olsson, p. 81; Preisigke, *Wörter.*, s.v. Cf. P.Oxy., IV. 729, 17f.; B.G.U., II. 614, 24.

14. ἕως οὗ (without ἄν): "until"; see Robertson, p. 976.

15–16. δοκῶ γάρ, συναιρόμενος πρὸς σὲ λογάριον παρεδεξάμην σοι πάντα. The editors wrongly punctuated with a comma after παραγένωμαι and a period after λογάριον. For the parataxis and the absolute use of δοκῶ cf. P.Oxy. IX. 1218, 7 ἡ μήτηρ μου Θαῆσις εἰς ᾿Αντινόου, δοκῶ, ἐπὶ κηδίαν ἀπῆλθεν, "my mother Thaesis went, I think, to Antinoöpolis for a funeral"; and 1 Cor. 4:9, δοκῶ γάρ, ὁ θεὸς . . . ἀπέδειξεν.

συναιρόμενος πρὸς σὲ λογάριον: "settling accounts with you." Cf. Matt. 18:23, συνᾶραι λόγον μετὰ τῶν δούλων αὐτοῦ. For the number of examples of συναίρω with λόγον in the sense of "settle accounts" see M.M. *Vocab.* s.v. See Robertson, p. 109; Deissmann, *Light*, p. 117; Moulton, *Proleg.*, p. 160.

παρεδεξάμην: For the use of this word in the sense of "to take care of an item in a budget account," see Olsson, p. 82.

17–19. παρακάλεσον . . . ἵνα ἐπιμέληται: ἵνα in a sub-final clause after ἐρωτῶ, παρακαλέω, etc. was formerly considered a Latinism. But in view of its frequent occurrence in the papyri it cannot be due to Latin influence. It is a natural development in the vernacular. See Robertson, pp. 991–4; see lines 3–4 above; cf. No. I. 13.

25. ἐπιστάτῃ: "agent." Aphrodisius was Ammonius' agent and friend. For the word see Preisigke, *Fach.*, and *Wörter.*, s.v.

# XIV

## CENSUS RETURN

### A.D. 48

P.Oxy. II. 255. Discovered and edited by Grenfell
and Hunt. Cf. Milligan, *Greek Papyri*, No. 17;
Wilcken, *Chrest.*, No. 201; P.S.I., Intro. to No. 53.

Δωρ[ίωνι σ]τρατηγῶι κ[αὶ . ]ην [ . . . . ]νω[ι
βα[σι]λικῷ γρ[α(μματεῖ)] καὶ Διδύμωι [καὶ . ] . [ . ] ο . ( )
τοπογρα(μματεῦσι) καὶ κωμογρα(μματεῦσι) παρὰ Θερ[μου-
θαρίου τῆς Θοώνιος μετὰ κυρίου
5 Ἀπολλω(νίου) τοῦ Σωτάδου. εἰσὶν
[οἱ] καταγεινόμενοι ἐν τῇ ὑπαρ-
χο[ύσῃ μοι οἰκίᾳ λαύρ]ας νότου [ . .

. . . . . . . . . . . . . . . .

Θερμου[θάριον ἀπελ(ευθέρα) τοῦ προ-
γ[εγ]ρα(μμένου) Σωτάδ[ου] ὡς (ἐτῶν) ξε,
10 μέση μελίχ(ρως) μακροπ(ρόσωπος) οὐλ(ὴ) γόνα(τι) δε[ξι]ῷ[ι.
(γίνονται) γ(υναῖκες) β.

Θερμουθάρι[ον] ἡ προγεγρα(μμένη) μ[ετὰ
κυρίου τοῦ α[ὐτο]ῦ Ἀπολλω(νίου) ὀμνύω
[Τ]ιβέριον Κλαύδιον Καίσαρα Σεβ[αστὸν
15 Γερμανικὸν Αὐτοκράτορα εἶ μὴν
[ἐ]ξ [ὑ]γιοῦς καὶ ἐπ' ἀληθείας ἐπι-
δεδωκέναι τὴ[ν π]ροκειμένην

[γρα]φὴν τῶν παρ' ἐμοὶ [ο]ἰκούν[των,
καὶ μηδένα ἕτερον οἰκ⟨ε⟩ῖν παρ' ἐμοὶ
20 μήτε ἐπ[ὶ]ξ[ενον μή]τε 'Αλεξανδ⟨ρέα⟩
μηδὲ ἀπελεύθερον μήτε 'Ρωμα⟨ῖο⟩ν
μηδὲ Αἰγύπ[τιον ἔ]ξ⟨ω⟩ τῶν προ-
γεγραμμένω[ν. εὐορ]κούσῃ μέν μοι
εὖ ε[ἴη, ἐφ]ιορκοῦντι δὲ τ[ὰ ἐν]αντία.
25 [ἔτο]υς ἐνάτου Τιβερίου Κλαυδ[ίου
[Καίσαρο]ς Σεβαστοῦ Γερμανικοῦ
[Αὐτοκρά]τορος, Φαῶφι[ . .

"To Dorion strategus and to . . . royal scribe
and to Didymus and . . . topogrammateis and
komogrammateis from Thermoutharion the daugh-
ter of Thoonis with her guardian Apollonius the son
of Sotades. The inhabitants of the house belonging
to me in the South Lane are . . . Thermoutharion, a
freedwoman of the aforesaid Sotades, about 65 years
(of age), of medium height, with honey-colored com-
plexion, having a long face, a scar on the right knee.
Total, two women.

I the aforesaid Thermoutharion with my guardian
the said Apollonius swear by Tiberius Claudius
Caesar Augustus Germanicus Emperor that I as-
suredly have honestly and truthfully presented the
preceding return of those living with me and that no
one else lives with me, neither a stranger, nor Alex-

andrian, nor freedman, nor Roman, nor Egyptian, except the aforesaid. If I am swearing truly, may it be well with me, but if falsely, the opposite.

The ninth year of Tiberius Claudius Caesar Augustus Germanicus Emperor, Phaophi. . . . "

[This papyrus is one of a large number of census returns or house-to-house enrolments (κατ' οἰκίαν ἀπογραφαί). An unusual degree of importance attaches to them because of the famous passage in Luke 2:1–4 respecting the enrolment held by Herod. See P.Oxy., II. pp. 207ff.; P.B.M., II. pp. 192ff.; Wilcken, *Greek Ostr.*, I. pp. 433ff.; *Chrest.* I. pp. 192ff.; Ramsay, *Was Christ Born in Bethlehem?* etc.]

1. στρατηγῶι: Iota adscript is frequent in first century papyri. See No. I, 1.

3. τοπογραμματεῦσι κτλ: The topogrammateis were scribes of the toparchies into which the nomes were divided. During the Roman period their functions tended to become merged in those of the komogrammateis (village scribes) who were subordinate officials. See Wilken, *Obs. ad hist. Aegypti*, pp. 23ff.; *Gr. Ostr.* I. pp. 428ff.; Editors' note P.Oxy. II. 251, 2.

4. κυρίου: "guardian," a legal term, of guardians for women, occurring many times in the papyri. See Archiv. IV. pp. 78ff.; V. pp. 471ff.

6. καταγεινόμενοι = καταγινόμενοι: ει = ι, see No.

VII, 15. For the meaning "live," "dwell," see LXX. Ex. 10:23.

8. Θερμουθάριον: The name of another woman (see line 11) must have been written in the space between line 7 and line 8. In the Fayum lists it is customary for the owner's name to come last.

ἀπελευθέρα: "feedwoman." If there were any slaves in the house, they were also included in the list; cf. B.G.U. 137, 10. For the word ἀπ. see 1 Cor. 7:22.

10. μέση: "middle height." In descriptions of personal characteristics the height came first.

μελίχρως: With an Egyptian "honey-colored" would be considered "fair."

13–23. ὀμνύω + name of the ruling Caesar . . . προγεγραμμένων. The phrases from verse 13 to 23 constitute, with the exception of εἰ μήν which occurs infrequently, a regular formula of oaths; cf. P.S.I. No. 53.

13. ὀμνύω followed by the acc. of the person invoked is regular in these oaths. Cf. James 5:12; see Robertson, p. 484.

15. εἰ μήν = ἦ μήν: For this term to give force of truthfulness to an assertion, see P.Oxy. II. 259, 6; 260, 7; P.B.M. II. 181, 13 (p. 147). See Heb. 6:14. For εἰ = η see Robertson, pp. 192, 1150; Mayser, I. pp. 74ff.

20. ἐπίξενον: "stranger"; this word was rare until

the publication of the census-returns in which it commonly occurs. It is found in an ostracon-receipt of A.D. 32–33 (Deissmann, *Light*, p. 111).

21. Ῥωμαῖον is the usual Greek form. The papyrus has Ρωμαν, the editors Ῥωμαν⟨όν⟩.

22. ἔξω: Many of the census-returns have παρέξ instead of ἔξω.

23. εὐορκούσῃ μέν μοι: "if I am swearing truly"; for this conditional use of the participle see Robertson, pp. 1022f., 1129.

24. εἴη: The optative is rare in vernacular Koine; it generally occurs in set phrases as here. See Robertson, pp. 325ff., 935f.; Mayser, I. p. 326; Jannaris, pp. 560ff.

ἐφιορκοῦντι is a breach in concord of gender; it should be in the feminine gender. See Robertson, p. 412. The form with ἐφ- is to be preferred to ἐπ-, because the form with ἐφ- is generally found in the papyri. The form with ἐπ- occurs in Matt. 5:33.

# XV

# LETTER OF MYSTARION TO STOTOETIS

### A.D. 50

B.G.U. I. 37. Edited by Fritz Krebs. Cf. Deissmann, *Light*, p. 170ff., *Bibelstudien*, p. 213; Olsson, pp. 96ff.

Μυσταρίων Στοτόητι τῶι
ἰδίωι πλεῖστα χαίρειν.
ἔπεμψα ὑμεῖν Βλάστον τὸν ἐμὸν
χάριν διχίλων ξύλων εἰς τοὺς
5 ἐλαιῶνάς μου. ὅρα οὖν μὴ αὐτὸν
κατάσχῃς. οἶδας γὰρ πῶς αὐτοῦ
ἐκάστης ὥρας χρήζωι.
*In another hand* ἔρρωσο.
(ἔτους) ια Τιβερίου Κλαυδίου Καίσαρος Σεβαστοῦ
10 Γερμ[α]νικο[ῦ] Αὐτοκράτορο[ς] μη(νὸς) Σεβα(στοῦ) ιε.
*On the verso (in the first hand)*
Στοτόητι λεσώνῃ εἰς τὴν νῆσον τ[ .

"Mystarion to his own Stotoetis many greetings.
I sent to you my Blastus about wooden forks for
my olive-orchards. See now that you do not detain
him. For you know how I need him every hour.
Good-bye.

The 11th year of Tiberius Claudius Caesar Augustus Germanicus Imperator, in the month Sebastus 15.

(Addressed)

To Stototis, chief priest, at the island ———."

1–2. τῶι ἰδίωι: "his own"; used here as a polite term of endearment; see Robertson, pp. 83, 691f.; Moulton, *Proleg.*, pp. 87ff. For the frequent iota adscript see No. I. 1. The phrase τῷ ἰδίῳ came into use along with others when the Roman republic changed into an empire; see Exler, pp. 31, 63.

3. ἔπεμψα: The epistolary aorist. See Robertson, pp. 845f. ὑμεῖν = ὑμῖν; for ει = ι see No. VII. 15.

4. χάριν: in the weakened sense of "about"; cf. P.Fay. 126, 5. In the N. T. it generally follows its noun, in the papyri it generally precedes the noun. See Robertson, p. 647.

διχίλων = διχήλων: "forks"; δίχηλος (adj.) is probably used here as a substantive. Cf. modern Greek. διχάλα = δικράνι, "fork," "rake." See Olsson, p. 97. For ι = η see Robertson, pp. 191f.; Mayser I. pp. 82f.

5. ἐλαιῶνας: For the word see No. VIII, 9.

5–6. ὅρα οὖν μὴ αὐτὸν κατάσχῃς: For ὅρα introducing prohibitions see Robertson, pp. 932f., 949; Horn, pp. 98, 102. In letters the recipient is often ordered not to detain the bearer of the letter; cf. B.G.U. IV. 1205, 26; P.Fay. 109, 11; P.Lille 18, 8–9. οὖν: transitional, see No. XIII, 7.

6–7. οἶδας γὰρ πῶς κτλ.: Here πῶς nearly = ὅτι; for

the encroachment of πῶς on ὅτι see Robertson, pp. 1032f., Blass-Debrunner, p. 223; Radamacher, p. 196.

7. χρήζωι: irrational iota, see No. I, 1.

8. ἔρρωσο: This concluding salutation is in a different hand than the rest of the letter. "St. Paul, we are told, has not in fact furnished all his letters with a salutation in his own hand, therefore the words 'which is the token in every letter' cannot be genuine." "We must not say," continues Deissmann, "that St. Paul only finished off with his own hand those letters in which he expressly says that he did. Mystarion's letter . . . was written only a few years before St. Paul's second letter to the Christians of Thessalonica, and it proves that somebody at that date closed a letter in his own hand without expressly saying so."—Deissmann, *Light*, p. 172.

10. λεσώνῃ: the title (λεσῶνις) of a priest in Egypt, who sometimes is given as chief administrator of a temple and sometimes as chief priest. See Preisigke, *Fach.* s.v.; *Wört.* s.v.

εἰς τὴν νῆσον: For the place of destination of a letter see Ziemann, pp. 281f. It is not known which island is here meant.

# XVI

## NOTICE OF DEATH

### A.D. 61

P.Oxy. II. 262. Discovered and edited by Grenfell and Hunt.

Φιλίσκωι ἐγλή(μπτορι) γερδ(ιακοῦ)
παρὰ Σαραπίωνος τοῦ Σαρα(πίωνος).
ὁ δοῦλός μου Ἀπολλοφάνης
γέρδιος ἀναγραφόμενος
5  ἐπ' ἀμφόδου Τεγμούθεως
ἐτελε(ύτησεν) ἐν τῆι ξένηι
τῶι ἐνεστῶτι ζ (ἔτει) Νέρωνο(ς)
Κλαυδίου Καίσαρος Σεβαστοῦ Γερμανι[κ(οῦ)
Αὐτοκράτορος. διὸ ἀξιῶ
10  ἀναγραφῆναι τοῦτον
ἐν τῆι τῶν τετελε(υτηκότων)
ἰάξει, καὶ ὀμνύωι
Νέρωνα Κλαύδιον Καίσαρ[α
Σεβαστὸν Γερμανικὸν Αὐτοκρά(τορα)
15  ἀληθῆι εἶναι.
(ἔτους) ζ Νέρωνος Κλαυδίου
Καίσαρος Σεβαστοῦ Γερμανικοῦ Αὐτοκρά(τορος)
Μεχ(εὶρ) κζ Σεβα(στῆ).
Second hand. Φιλίσκος σεσημ(είωμαι).

20 (ἔτους) ζ Νέρωνος Κλαυδίου

[Κα]ίσαρος Σεβαστοῦ

[Γερ]μανικοῦ

[Αὐτο]κράτορ[ος,

[Με]χ(είρ) κζ [Σεβα(στῇ).

.  .  .  .  .  .  .  .  .  .  .

"To Philiscus, collector of the tax on weaving, from Serapion, son of Serapion.

My slave Apollophanes a weaver, registered in Temgenouthis Square, died away from home in the present 7th year of Nero Claudius Caesar Augustus Germanicus Imperator. Wherefore I request that he be enrolled in the roll of the dead, and I swear by Nero Claudius Caesar Augustus Germanicus Imperator that the above statements are true.

The 7th year of Nero Claudius Caesar Augustus Germanicus Imperator, Mecheir 27, dies Augusta.

I, Philiscus, have signed."

*Repetition of the date.*

1. ἐγλήμπτορι = ἐκλήμπτορι: "collector of taxes," "farmer of taxes." For assimilation of κ to γ see Mayser, I. p. 227.

γερδιακοῦ (sc. τέλους): Both the adjective and the substantive γέρδιος (line 4) occur frequently in the papyri, though rare elsewhere.

5. ἀμφόδου: "square," the regular word in the papyri for a "quarter" or "block" of a city. In the

N. T. it occurs only in Mk. 11:4 and in the text of D in Acts 19:28.

Τεγμούθεως: It is spelled five different ways in various papyri, the name of an ἄμφοδον at Oxyrhynchus.

6. ἐν τῆι ξένηι: "away from home;" in the papyri frequently means merely any place outside the nome in which a person was registered.

9. ἀξιῶ: see VIII. 14.

12. τάξει: τάξις is found frequently in the papyri with the meaning "list," "roll."

καὶ ὀμνύωι: Irrational iota. See No. XIV, 13–23 for the regular phrase in oaths.

15. ἀληθῆι εἶναι: with these words is generally found the phrase τὰ προγεγραμμένα or its like. The iota in ἀλ. is irrational.

18. Σεβαστῆ: ἡμέραι Σεβασταί were certain days named to commemorate the birthday or the accession of the ruling emperor and his predecessors or possibly one of the emperor's family. See P.Ryl. II. p. 142; Blumenthal, *Archiv*, V. pp. 336ff.

# XVII

## INVITATION FROM DIDYMUS TO APOLLONIUS

A.D. 84

B.G.U. II. 596. Edited by Fritz Krebs. See Milligan,
*Greek Papyri*, pp. 63f.; Olsson, pp. 142f. Erman-Krebs,
*Aus den Papyrus der Kgl. Museen*, p. 217; Schubart,
*Ein Jahrtausend am Nil*, 53.

Δίδυμος Ἀπολλωνίωι
τῶι τιμιωτάτωι
χαίρειν.

καλῶς ποιήσεις συνελθὼν
5 [Α]ἰλουρίωνι τῶι κομίζον-
τί σοι τὸ ἐπ[ι]στ[ό]λιον, ὅπως
εἰς τὴν ἑορτὴν περιστε-
ρείδια ἡμεῖν ἀγοράσηι,
καὶ ἐρωτηθεὶς κατελ-
10 θὼν συνευωχηθῇ[ς]
ἡμεῖν. τοῦτ[ο] οὖν ποιή-
σας ἔσῃ μοι μεγάλην
χάριταν κατ[α]τεθειμ[έ]νο(ς).
ἄσπασαι τοὺς σοὺς πάντας.
15    ἔρρωσο.

(ἔτους) τρίτου Αὐτοκράτορος
Καίσαρος Δομιτιανοῦ

Σεβαστοῦ Γερμανικοῦ Παχ(ὼν) ιε.

*On the verso*

20 εἰς Βακχιάδα [ἀπόδος Ἀπολλωνίωι] τῶι τιμιωτ[ά(τωι)].

"Didymus to his most esteemed Apollonius greeting. Please accompany Ailourion, who brings the note to you, in order that he may buy for us young pigeons for the feast, and that you being invited may come down and feast together with us. If then you do this, you will have conferred upon me a great favor. Greet all yours. Good-bye.

The third year of Emperor Caesar Domitian Augustus Germanicus, Pachon 15.

(Addressed)

Deliver at Bacchias to the most esteemed Apollonius."

1-3. The opening greeting of this type with τῷ τιμιωτάτῳ (which came into use when the Roman republic changed into an empire) is common from the first century A.D. to the third century A.D. See Exler, pp. 30f.; 62f. For iota adscript with τῶι τιμιωτάτωι see No. I, 1.

4. καλῶς ποιήσεις: "please," "you will do well," "be so good as." This phrase commonly introduces a polite command or request, and is usually followed by the aorist participle of coincident action as here; but see No. XII, 11-12. Cf. Meecham, *Light*, pp. 122f.

συνελθών: This word is used in Luke 23:55 and Acts 9:39 in the sense of "go with," "accompany."

5–6. τῶι κομίζοντι: This is also a regular phrase, as well as ὁ ἀποδιδούς, for "the bearer" of a letter. Cf. No. V, 3. See also No. VII, 3.

7. ἑωρτήν = ἑορτήν: For the confusion of ω and ο see Robertson, p. 200; Mayser, I, pp. 97ff.

7–8. περιστερείδια = περιστερίδια: "young pigeons"; this diminutive occurs eight or nine times in the papyri. For ει = ι see No. VII, 15.

8. ἡμεῖν = ἡμῖν: ει = ι, see above.

9. ἐρωτηθείς: may also = "please" from the meaning "having been asked what one's pleasure is"; cf. P.Oxy. II. 269, 4. For ἐρωτάω see No. I, 6.

9–10. κατελθών: Apollonius lived in the town of Bacchias in the Fayum, and in all probability Didymus lived southwest of Bacchias.

10. συνευωχηθῆς: Cf. 2 Peter 2:13, συνευωχούμενοι ὑμῖν.

11. ἡμεῖν = ἡμῖν: See line 8 above.

ποιήσας: "if you do this"; for the conditional use of the participle see Robertson, p. 1129. Cf. No. XV, 23; see P.Tebt. I, 56, 15 (2nd Cent. B.C.).

12–13. ἔσῃ μοι μεγάλην χάριταν κατατεθειμένος: For the classical phrase χάριν κατατίθημι in the N. T. see Acts 24:27; 25:9. For the double accusative ending (-α plus ν) in χάριταν (= χάριτα) see Robertson, pp. 258, 264f. The papyri show χάριν as the general rule in the Ptolemaic period, in the Roman period and interchange between χάριν and χάριτα. See Mayser, I. pp. 271f.; Crönert, *Mem. Gr. Hercul.*, p. 170.

For the periphrastic future perfect, ἔση κατατεθει-μένος see Robertson, p. 361; Mayser, 377. Cf. ἔση κεχαρισμένος, P.Oxy., VII. 1060, 20 (B.C. 22); P.Tebt. I. 56, 16 (130–120 B.C.); cf. Witkowski, *Ep. Pr. Gr.*, p. 99, note 16.

19. Concerning the address see lines 9–10 above, and Ziemann, pp. 282f.

# XVIII

## LETTER FROM GEMELLUS TO SABINUS

### A.D. 100

P.Fay. 114. From the Fayum. Edited by Grenfell and
Hunt. See Olsson, p. 164.

Λούκιος Βελλῆνος Γέμελλος
Σαβίνωι τῶι οιειῶι χαίρειν.
εὖ οὖν πυήσας κομισάμε-
νός μου τὴν ἐπιστολὴν
5 πέμσις μυ Πίνδαρον
εἰς τὴν πόλιν τὸν πεδι-
οφύλακα τῆς Διονυσιάδο(ς),
ἐπὶ ἐρώτησέ με Ἑρμῶ-
ναξ εἴνα αὐτὸν λά-
10 βῃ εἰς Κερκεσοῦχα
καταμαθῖν τὸν
ἐλαιῶνα αὐτοῦ ἐπὶ
πυκνός ἐστιν καὶ
θέλι ἐξ αὐτὸν ἐκκο-
15 ψαι φυτά, εἴνα ἐνπί-
ρος κοπῇ τὰ μέλλον-
τα ἐκκόπτεσθαι · καὶ
τὴν εἰκθυὶν πέμσις
τῆι κδ εἴ κε εἰς τὰ

20   γενέσια Γεμέλλης.

   μὴ ο⟨ὖ⟩ν ληρήσῃς τὸν

   ἐκτιναγμόν σου.

   ἔρρωσο. (ἔτους) δ Αὐτοκράτορος

   Καίσαρος Νερούα

25   Τραιαν[οῦ] Σεβαστοῦ

   Γερμανικοῦ, Χύακ

     ιη.

"Lucius Bellenus Gemellus to his son Sabinus, greeting. On receipt of my letter you will, please, send to the city to me Pindarus, the field guard at Dionysias; for Hermonax asked me that he might take him to Kerkesucha to examine his olive-orchard as it is thickly grown and he wishes to cut out some of the trees, in order that those which are going to be cut out may be expertly cut. And you shall send the fish on the 24th or 25th for Gemella's birthday feast. Don't talk nonsense about your winnowing. Good-bye. The 4th year of the Emperor Caesar Nerva Trajanus Augustus Germanicus, Choiak 18."

1. Γέμελλος was a large landowner in the Fayum. Most of his farms, in which he took a keen interest, were situated near Euhemeria. This letter is one of fourteen of a family budget. For the most part they are written by Gemellus who was head of the family and sixty years of age in 100 A.D. (date of present

letter). Concerning his handwriting and grammar the editors write: "But it (handwriting) was perhaps never very good, any more than his spelling and grammar, which are peculiarly atrocious." "The general impression of Gemellus left by these letters is that of a shrewd old man of business, somewhat wilful and exacting, but of a kind and generous disposition."

2. τῶι οιειῶι = τῷ υἱῷ: For iota adscript see No. I, 1; οι = υ, see Robertson, p. 198. Mayser, I. p. 111; for ει = ι see Robertson, pp. 195ff.; Mayser, I. pp. 87ff.

3–5. εὖ οὖν πυήσας (= ποιήσας) ... πέμσις (= πέμψεις): For this construction see No. XII, 11–12 and No. XVII, 4. For itacism, ι = ει, υ = οι see line 2 above.

5. μυ = μοι: υ = οι, see references in line 2 above for interchange of vowels.

6–7. τὸν πεδιοφύλακα: There were both private and public field-guards.

8. ἐπί = ἐπεί: For ι = ει see Robertson, pp. 195ff.; Mayser, I. pp. 87ff.

ἐρώτησε = ἠρώτησε: The writer may have felt that ἐ was in sound the temporal augment. See Jannaris, pp. 81, 188; and cf. ῥωτῶ (= ἐρωτῶ) since 1000 A.D. Cf. Robertson, pp. 366f.; Mayser, I. p. 336.

8–9. Ἑρμῶναξ = Ἑρμῶναξ: ο = ω, see Robertson, p. 200; Mayser, I. pp. 132–7.

εἶνα = ἵνα: ει = ι, see line 2 above.

9–10. εἶνα αὐτὸν λάβῃ: For the construction ἵνα +

subjunctive after ἐρωτάω see Robertson, p. 993, 1046. See No. I, 6, 13.

10. Κερκεσοῦχα: a village in the district of Heraclides.

11. καταμαθῖν = καταμαθεῖν: "to examine," "to inspect." For ι = ει, see line 8 above.

12. ἐλαιῶνα: see No. VIII, 9.

ἐπί = ἐπεί: see line 8 above.

14. θέλι = θέλει: For ι = ει, see line 8 above.

ἐξ αὐτὸν = ἐξ αὐτῶν: ο = ω, see lines 8–9 above. For the partitive use of ἐκ, see Robertson, p. 599.

15. εἵνα = ἵνα: see line 9 above.

15–16. ἐνπίρος = ἐνπείρως = ἐμπείρως: For ι = ει, see line 8 above; ο = ω, lines 8–9 above. For non-assimilation of ν, see Robertson, p. 216, Mayser, I. p. 233.

16–17. Here μέλλω is followed by the present (passive) infinitive. Cf. Robertson, p. 1081.

18. εἰκθυίν = ἰχθύν: ει = ι, see line 2 above; υι = υ, see Jannaris, pp. 45, 48; Mayser, I, pp. 112f. For κ in place of χ, see Mayser, I. p. 172.

πέμσις = πέμψεις: See lines 3–5 above.

19. εἴ = ἤ: For ει = η, see Robertson, p. 192; Mayser, I. p. 78.

20. γενέσια: This word in the Koine came to mean the birthday feast of a living person. Cf. Mt. 4:6; Mk. 6:21.

22. ἐκτιναγμόν may refer to the "shaking down," harvesting, of figs.

# XIX

## LETTER OF HORUS TO APION

LATE FIRST CENTURY

P.Oxy., II. 299. Discovered and edited by Grenfell and Hunt. See Laudien, *Gr. Papyri*, pp. 8, 40f.; Olsson, *Papyrusbriefe*, pp. 207f.; Hunt and Edgar, *Select Papyri*, pp. 298f.

Ὧρος Ἀπίωνι τῷ τειμειωτάτωι χαίρειν.

Λάμπωνι μυοθηρευτῇ ἔδωκα αὐτῷ διὰ σοῦ ἀραβῶνα (δραχμὰς) η ἵνα μυοθηρεύσει ἐν Τόκα. καλῶς ποιήσεις
πέμψεις μοι αὐτάς. καὶ Διονυσίῳ προσ[τ]άτῃ Νεμερῶν
κέκρηκα (δραχμὰς) η καὶ ταύτας οὐκ ἔπεμψε, ἵνα εἰδῇς.
    ἔρρωσ(ο).    Παῦνι κδ.

"Horus to his most esteemed Apion greeting. To Lampon the mouse-catcher I gave (to him) for you 8 drachmae as earnest money that he may catch mice in Toka. You will please send them (8 drachmae) to me. And I have lent Dionysius, the chief man of Nemerae, 8 drachmae, and he has not sent them; (I write) in order that you may know it.

Good-bye. Pauni 24."

1. τειμειωτάτωι = τιμωτάτῳ: For itacism, ει = ι, see No. XVIII, 2. For iota adscript see No. I, 1.

2. Λάμπωνι . . . ἔδωκα αὐτῷ: The redundant per-

sonal pronoun αὐτῷ is exactly paralleled in Rev. 2:7, 17, τῷ νικῶντι δώσω αὐτῷ. Such pleonasm of the oblique cases of the personal pronouns is common in the vernacular Koine. See Robertson, p. 683; Blass-Debrunner, pp. 6, 160, 170.

μυοθηρευτῇ and μυοθηρεύσει are rare words.

διὰ σοῦ: It seems that from the context this phrase must be taken as practically meaning "on your account" (= ὑπὲρ σοῦ). For the use of διά + gen. or acc. = "on account of," "for the sake of," that later supplanted ὑπέρ + ablative, see Sophocles, Lex. s.v.; Jannaris, pp. 373ff.

2–3. ἀραβῶνα: "earnest money." There are many instances of this word in the paypri with the N. T. meaning (as here) of "a part given in advance (in guarantee of what is to follow)." It is an everyday business term. Cf. the Latin arrhabo, arrha. As to spelling, ἀρραβών and ἀραβών are about equally frequent. See Robertson, pp. 81, 105, 212.

3. ἵνα μυοθηρεύσει: ἵνα + the future indicative in pure final clauses occurs a number of times in the papyri. See Robertson, pp. 984, 1413. Of course itacism (ει = η) is possible, but not probable here.

ἐν Τόκα: a village. The editors first had ἔντοκα. Literary writers as well as the papyri mention the great number of mice in Egypt. Cf. Diodarus, I. 10, 2; Herodotus, II. 141. Cf. P.Grenf. II. pp. 36, 15f.;

ἠκούσαμεν τὸν μῦν καταβεβρωκέναι τὸν σπόρον, "we heard that the mice have eaten up the crop."

3–4. καλῶς ποιήσεις πέμψεις: see No. XVIII, 3–5.

4. αὐτάς: antecedent is δραχμὰς η.

5. κέκρηκα = κέχρηκα: from κιχράω or κίχρημι. For interchange of κ and χ see Mayser, I. p. 172.

6. ἵνα εἰδῇς: This phase is frequent in the papyri; see Horn, pp. 33f. There is in all probability an ellipsis of a verb such as γράφω or θέλω before ἵνα; cf. P.S.I. pp. 377, 19, ἔγραψα οὖν σοι ἵνα εἰδῆις.

# XX

## QUESTION TO THE ORACLE

### FIRST CENTURY A.D.

P.Fay. 137. Edited by Grenfell and Hunt. See Milligan, *Greek Papyri*, pp. 68f.; Wilcken, *Chrest.*, I. p. 149.

Σοκωννωκοννῖ θεῶι με⟨γά⟩λο μεγάλωι. χρημάτισόν μοι, ἢ μείνωι
ἐν Βακχιάδι; ἢ μέλ⟨λ⟩ω ἐντυνχάνιν; τούτωι ἐμοὶ χρημάτισον.

"To Sokanobkoneus the great, great god. Give me an answer, Shall I remain in Bacchias? Am I going to meet (him?)? Answer me this."

1. Σοκωννωκοννῖ = Σοκανοβκονεῖ (as it is correctly spelled in P.Fay. 18, 3): the local deity of the town of Bacchias. The word is probably a compound of Σοκ (Sebek) ανοβ (Anubis) + κοννευς (meaning uncertain). The crocodile god Sebek was the nome god of the Fayum. The practice of addressing questions to local deities in times of difficulty seems to have been widespread.

1–2. θεῶι μεγάλο μεγάλωι = θεῷ μεγάλῳ μεγάλῳ: The repetition of the adjective gives the sense of an elative superlative. See Robertson, p. 660. Cf. P.Tebt.,

I. 63, 5, θεοῦ μεγάλου μεγάλου. For iota adscript see No. I, 1.

2. χρημάτισον: What relation there is, if any, between χρηματίζω, "transact business," "get a name from," and χρηματίζω, "give answer," "instruct," "warn," is not evident. In the LXX it is frequently used of a divine response (as here) or command; in N. T. cf. Matt. 2:12.

ᾖ μείνωι (= μείνω): the deliberative subjunctive; see Robertson, pp. 934f. The delib. subj. is not frequent in the papyri; see Horn, pp. 89f.; Mayser, II. pp. 235f. It is used either in direct or in indirect questions. For irrational iota see No. I, 1. It is possible that ᾖ = εἰ.

3–4. ἐντυνχάνιν = ἐντυγχάνειν: For ν before χ, see Mayser, pp. 235f.; Robertson, p. 216f. For ι = ει, see No. XVIII, 5.

4. τούτωι = τοῦτο: For ωι written in place of ο see Mayser, I. p. 137; see Robertson, p. 200.

# XXI

## LETTER OF THEON TO SARAPOUS

### LATE FIRST CENTURY A.D.

P.Oxy., VIII. 1154. Discovered and edited by Grenfell and Hunt. See Olsson, *Papyrusbriefe*, pp. 209f.

Θέ[ω]ν Σαραποῦτι τῇ ἀδελφῇ
　　χαίρειν.
πρὸ πάντων ὡς ἐνετει-
λάμην σοι κατ' ὄψιν ἐπιμέ-
5　λου σεαυτῆς ἵνα μοι ὑγιαι-
νῃς· μὴ ἀγωνιάσῃς δὲ
περὶ ἐμοῦ ὅτι ἐπὶ ξένης εἰμί, αὐτόπτης γὰρ εἰμὶ
τῶν τόπων καὶ οὐκ εἰμὶ
10　ξέν[ο]ς τῶν ἐνθάδε. ἐὰν
　[δὲ σ]τρατεύσ[ωμαι (?)

　.　.　.　.　.　.　.　.　.　.　.　.

*In the left hand margin, at right angles*
πατέρα σου καὶ τὴν ματέρα καὶ τοὺς ἀδε[λφοὺς
[ . . . . . . . . . . . ] . [ . . . ] . . σίον 'Αρσινοείτου [
*On the verso*
　　　　π̣[(αρὰ)] Θέωνος　[

"Theon to his sister Sarapous, greeting. Above all things, as I enjoined upon you in person, take care

76

of yourself that you may keep well for me; and do
not get anxious about me because I am away from
home, for I am personally acquainted with the
places and I am not a stranger to the people here.
Now if I become a soldier . . .

(In the margin)

(Salute) your father and mother and brothers.

(On the verso)          From Theon."

1. τῇ ἀδελφῇ: "sister" and probably wife; see No.
I, 1.

3–6. πρὸ πάντων . . . ὑγιαίνῃς: This is a combi-
nation of an opening and a closing phrase in familiar
letters; see Ziemann, p. 318; but Exler, pp. 113ff.,
treats this phrase as a final phrase in familiar letters.
Cf. No. V, 11. See P.Oxy., II, pp. 294, 30–31.

4. κατ' ὄψιν: "in person," face to face. Cf. P.Oxy.
I, 117, 3, κατ' ὄψιν σε παρακέκληκα, "I have urged you
in person."

4–5. ἐπιμέλου σεαυτῆς: ἐπιμέλομαι is found in the
N. T. with the genitive as here; but it is used also
with the dative, see No. I, 6–7.

5–6. ἵνα μοι ὑγιαίνῃς: ἵνα + the subjunctive after
ἐπιμέλομαι (ἐπιμελέομαι) is supplanting ὅπως + the subj.
Horn, p. 32, says: "Among the examples of purpose
I have placed the phrase ἐπιμέλου σεαυτοῦ ἵνα (ὅπως)
ὑγιαίνῃς, although it approaches an object clause very
closely. It is common in letters of the Ptolemaic

period and continues into the 1st century A.D. The examples with ὅπως all belong to the Ptolemaic age. The proportion seems to be ἵνα: ὅπως : : 30:4. ἵνα is decidedly preferred in this phrase." See Jannaris, 458; Mayser, II. pp. 242f.; Robertson, pp. 982ff., 985f., 994.

6. μὴ ἀγωνιάσῃς: For the verb see No. I, 13.

7. ἐπὶ ξένης: This phrase in the papyri is common in the sense of "away from home"; see the word in No. XVI, 6.

8. αὐτόπτης: "eye-witness," "personally acquainted with." Used once in N. T., Luke 1:2. Cf. P.Giss., 68, 17, ἐπὶ (= ἐπεὶ) Φιβᾶs . . . ἄπειρός ἐστιν τῶν τόπων "for Phibas is unacquainted with the places."

10. ἐνθάδε: "here." See Robertson, pp. 299, 548; Blass-Debrunner, p. 62. For the article with adverbs see Robertson, pp. 765f.

12. The editors (G. and H.) suggest that ἀσπάζου (or ἀσπάζομαι) τόν preceded πατέρα.

# INDEX OF GREEK WORDS

# INDEX OF GREEK WORDS

*The references are to documents and lines or notes on documents.*

ἀβασκάντως V, 12
ἄγω X, 16
ἀγωνιάω I, 4; XXI, 6
ἀδελφή I, 1; XXI, 1
ἀδελφός VII, 18
ἀήρ XII, 14–15
αἱρέομαι VI, 5
αἴτιος X, 16–17
ἀκούω XIX, 3
ἀλήθεια VII, 11–12
ἀληθής XVI, 15
ἄλλος VII, 18
ἄμφοδον XVI, 5
ἀμφότεροι IV, 3
ἄν VI, 3
ἀναβολή IX, 10–11
ἀναδίδωμι V, 3
ἀξιόω VIII, 14; XVI, 6
ἄπειρος XXI, 8
ἀπελεύθερος XIV, 8
ἀπέρχομαι XIII, 15–16
ἀπέχω III, 3; IV, 4, 12
ἀποδείκνυμι XIII, 15–16
ἀποδίδωμι I, 15; V, 3; XVII, 5–6
ἀποχή X, 14
ἀρ(ρ)αβών XIX, 2–3
ἄρσενον I, 9
ἄρσην I, 9
ἀρτάβη XIII, 8, 10
ἀρτίδιον II, 8
ἀρχέφοδος X, 15

ἀσπάζομαι VII, 7; XXI, 12
αὐτόπτης XXI, 8

βασιλεύς IX, 16
βλάβος VIII, 13
βούλομαι VI, 5
βραδύς IV, 9

γενέσια XVIII, 20
γένημα III, 3; IV, 5
γέννημα III, 5
γερδιακός XVI, 1
γέρδιος XVI, 1
γεωργός X, 7–8
γίνομαι III, 5, 8
γινώσκω XI, 2
γράμμα III, 10, 11; V, 6
γραπτός V, 8
γράφω III, 10; IV, 7, 9; V, 5; XI,
    8–9; XII, 11–12; XIII, 3–4;
    XIX, 6

δεῖπνον II, 1
δέομαι VIII, 14
δέσμη X, 11
δέω X, 17
διά XIX, 2
δίδωμι V, 3; X, 13; XIII, 3–4;
    XIX, 2
δίκαιος VI, 4
δίκρανος XV, 4

διμνώου III, 7
διοικητής V, 14
δίχηλος XV, 4
δοκέω XIII, 15–16
δοῦλος XIII, 15–16
δραχμή XII, 5; XIX, 4
δύναμαι IX, 23–25
δυσί III, 3; IV, 3

ἐάν I, 7, 9–10; VI, 3, 5; IX, 13, 23–25
ἑαυτοῦ, -ῆς XI, 5–6
ἐάω XII, 11–12
ἔδαφος X, 7
εἰ μήν XIV, 15
εἰμί I, 4; XIV, 24
εἴρηκα I, 11
εἰς VI, 4–5; XV, 4
ἐκ XIII, 9; XVIII, 14
ἐκβάλλω I, 10
ἐκεῖ VII, 5
ἐκλήμπτωρ XVI, 1
ἐκλογιστής IX, 11–12
ἐλαιών VIII, 9; XV, 5; XVIII, 12
ἐμβαίνω XI, 6
ἐμός VI, 4–5
ἐμπείρως XVIII, 15–16
ἐνθάδε XXI, 10
ἐνίστημι X, 5
ἐντέλλω XIII, 3–4
ἐντυγχάνω XX, 3–4
ἔξοδος X, 17
ἔξω XIV, 22
ἑορτή XVII, 7
ἐπακολουθέω VIII, 13
ἐπί XXI, 7
ἐπιβάλλω VIII, 6; X, 6
ἐπιγινώσκω XII, 14–15

ἐπιλανθάνω I, 11, 12–13
ἐπιμέλομαι I, 6–7; XIII, 17–19; XXI, 4–5
ἐπίξενος XIV, 20
ἐπισημασία V, 10
ἐπισπουδαστής III, 2
ἐπιστάτης VIII, 1; XIII, 25
ἐπιστολή V, 6; VII, 3
ἔρχομαι XI, 8–9
ἐρωτάω I, 6; V, 7; VI, 1; XIII, 17–19; XVII, 9; XVIII, 8
ἔσομαι VIII, 16–17; X, 17
ἕτερος XIII, 6
εὖ V, 12–13; XVIII, 3–5
εὐθύς I, 7
εὐορκέω XIV, 23
εὐτυχέω VIII, 18; X, 18
εὔχομαι V, 11, 12–13
ἐφιορκέω XIV, 24
ἔχω VII, 5–6
ἕως οὗ XIII, 14

ἡδέως IX, 23–25
ἡμέρα XII, 3; XVI, 18
ἡμέτερος VI, 1
ἦν I, 9–10

θέλω VI, 5; XVIII, 14; XIX, 6
θεός XX, 1–2
θῆλυς I, 10
θρίδαξ II, 6

ἴδιος III, 1; XV, 1–2
ἵνα I, 13; XIII, 3–4, 17–19; XVIII, 9–10, 15; XIX, 3, 6; XXI, 5–6
ἰχθύς XVIII, 18

καλλιότερος XII, 6
καλῶς XII, 11–12; XVII, 4; XIX, 3–4
Κανωπικός II, 2
καταγίνομαι XIV, 4
καταλογή VI, 4–5
καταμανθάνω XVIII, 11
κατατίθημι XVIII, 12–13
κατέρχομαι XVII, 9–10
κατέχω XV, 5–6
καυχάομαι V, 9
κιχράω XIX, 5
κίχρημι XIX, 5
κομίζω VII, 3; XVII, 5–6
κυρία I, 3
κύριος I, 3; XIV, 4
κωμογραμματεύς IX, 8

λαμβάνω VI, 5; IX, 14; XVIII, 9–10
λεῖος XII, 5
λεσῶνις XV, 10
ληστρικός VIII, 6–7; X, 7
λογάριον XIII, 15–16
λόγος IV, 4; IX, 16; XIII, 15–16
λοιπόν IX, 13

μέγας XVIII, 12–13; XIX, 1–2
μελίχρως XIV, 10
μέλλω XVIII, 16–17
μένω XX, 2
μερίς VIII, 8–9; X, 9
μέρος VIII, 15
μέσος XIV, 10
μετά V, 5
μή I, 4, 11; VII, 5–6; XXI, 6
μήν IV, 10
μήτηρ XI, 1; XIII, 15–16

μονοδεσμία X, 11
μυοθηρευτής XIX, 2
μυοθηρεύω XIX, 2–3

νῆσος XV, 10
νικάω XIX, 2
νύξ VIII, 3; X, 3–7

ξένη XVI, 6; XXI, 7

οἶδα III, 11; XV, 6–7; XIX, 6
οἰνάριον XII, 5
ὀλίγος VIII, 11, 13
ὅλως I, 4
ὀμνύω XIV, 13–23; XVI, 12
ὁμολογέω IX, 10
ὄνος X, 11; XII, 19–20
ὅπως X, 14; XXI, 5–6
ὁράω XV, 5–6
ὅς VI, 3; IX, 4; X, 7
ὅτι I, 11; XV, 6–7
οὖν IX, 13; XIII, 7; XV, 5–6; XVIII, 3–5
οὗτος XX, 4
ὀψαρίδιον VII, 13–14
ὀψάριον VII, 13–14
ὄψις XXI, 4
ὀψώνιον I, 7–8

παρά XII, 14–15
παραβάλλω VII, 5
παραδέχομαι XIII, 15–16
παραιτέομαι V, 6
παρακαλέω V, 5; XIII, 17–19
παρέξ XIV, 22
πᾶς XIII, 9, 15–16; XX, 3–6
πατήρ XXI, 12
πεδιοφύλαξ XVIII, 6–7

πέμπω XV, 3; XVIII, 3–5; XIX, 3–4
περί VI, 5; VIII, 15
περιστερίδιον XVII, 7–8
πίομαι V, 9
πλειστάκι VIII, 12
ποιέω VI, 4–5; IX, 10–11; XII, 11–12; XVII, 4, 11; XVIII, 3–5; XIX, 3–4
πολλαπολλῶν I, 9
πράττω V, 12–13
πράσσω XII, 3
προγράφω XIV, 13–23; XVI, 15
προκιχράω XIII, 13–14
προκίχρημι XIII, 13–14
προσέρχομαι VI, 3
προστάτης III, 1; IV, 1
προστάτις III, 1
πρόσωπον XII, 4
προφήτης VIII, 2
πτέρυξ II, 10
πῶς XV, 6–7

ῥώννυμι V, 12–13; XV, 8

Σεβαστός IV, 10
σημεῖον V, 8
σιναπηρός VII, 14
σιτευτός II, 9
σιτιστός II, 9
σπόρος XIX, 3
στρατηγός X, 1; XIV, 1
συναίρω XIII, 15–16
συνέρχομαι XVII, 4
συνευωχέω XVII, 10
συνίστημι V, 6; VI, 1
συστατικός V, 6

τάξις XVI, 12
τίμιος V, 1; XVII, 1–3; XIX, 1
τὶς X, 6
τοπογραμματεύς XIV, 2
τόπος VIII, 8; XXI, 8
τραπεζίτης IX, 16
τριάκοντα X, 12
τρόπον XIII, 9
τρόπος VIII, 6–7

ὑγιαίνω V, 11, 12; IX, 4; XII, 2; XXI, 3–6
ὑγιής XIV, 13–23
ὑπάγω XI, 8–9
ὑπέρ III, 10; IV, 7; VI, 5; VIII, 15; XIX, 2
υἱός XVIII, 2

φάγομαι V, 9
φαίνω VIII, 14
φάσις IX, 16
φέρω VIII, 3; X, 3
φιλέω VII, 7
φυλακίτης VIII, 1

χαίρω I, 2; III, 3; IV, 4; V, 2; XI, 1
χαρίζω V, 9
χάριν XV, 4
χάρις XII, 5–6; XVII, 12–13
χρήζω XV, 7
χρηματίζω XX, 2
χρηστός VII, 16
χώρα V, 14

ᾧδε XI, 4
ὡς IX, 16
ὥστε IX, 16

2. ? GIOVANNI BELLINI

5. BOCCACCIO BOCCACCINO

7 *recto.* STYLE OF BOTTICELLI

8 *recto*. VITTORE CARPACCIO

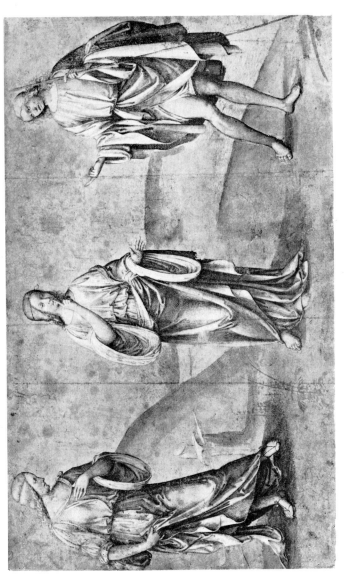

10.  FRANCESCO FRANCIA

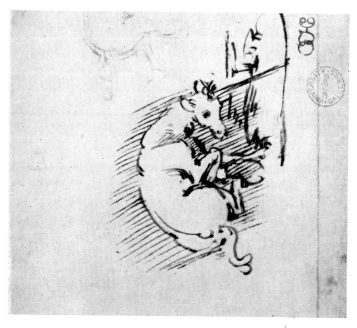

15, 16. LEONARDO DA VINCI

18. LEONARDO DA VINCI

21. FILIPPINO LIPPI

22. FRA FILIPPO LIPPI

25. BARTOLOMEO MONTAGNA

27. PIETRO PERUGINO

32. CIRCLE OF PERUGINO

40. ? BERNARDINO PINTORICCHIO

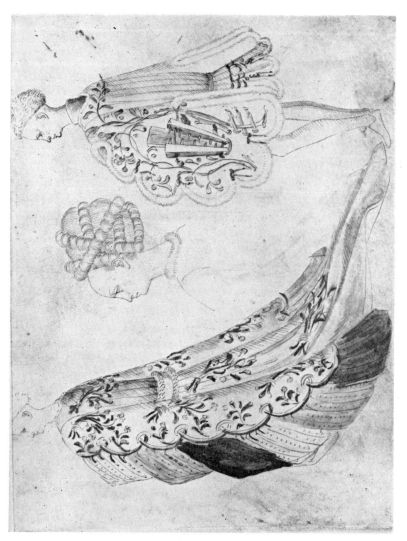

41 *verso*. ANTONIO PISANELLO

43. LORENZO SALIMBENI

46. TIMOTEO VITI

48. ANONYMOUS:? NORTH ITALIAN, EARLY SIXTEENTH CENTURY

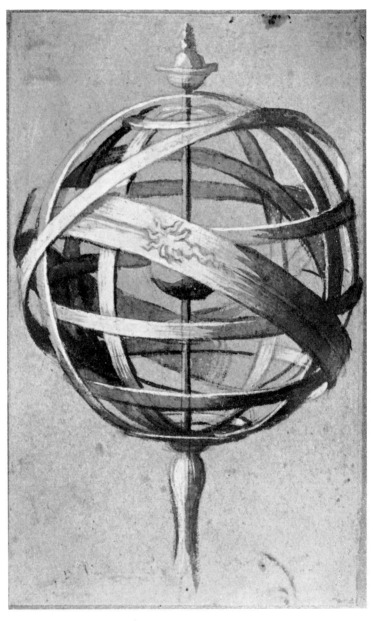

50. ANONYMOUS: ? VENETIAN, EARLY SIXTEENTH CENTURY

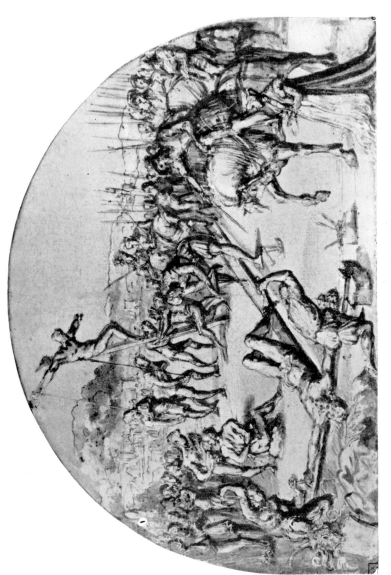

53. ANONYMOUS: NORTH ITALIAN, MID-SIXTEENTH CENTURY

64. NICCOLÒ DEL ABBATE

65. NICCOLÒ DEL ABBATE

70. GIOVANNI ALBERTI

77. BACCIO BANDINELLI

93. FEDERIGO BAROCCI

94. FEDERIGO BAROCCI

96. FEDERIGO BAROCCI

103. FRA BARTOLOMMEO

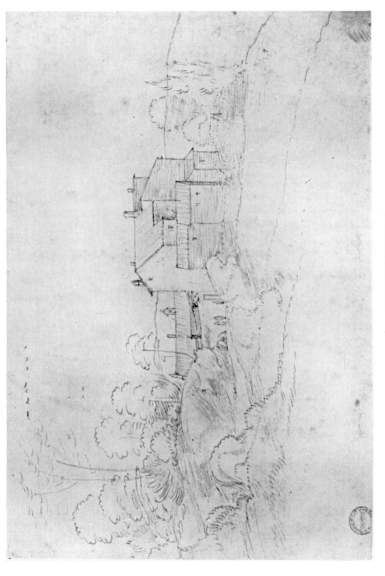

106. FRA BARTOLOMMEO

110. JACOPO BASSANO

112. LEANDRO BASSANO

116. ? GIOVANNI FRANCESCO BEZZI

117. CAMILLO BOCCACCINO

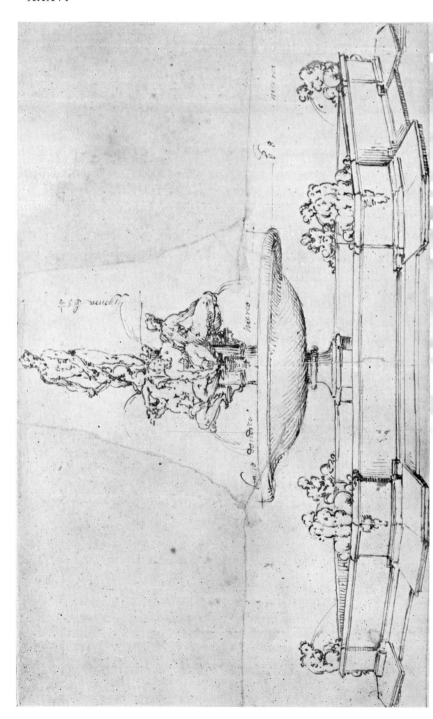

120. PARIS BORDONE

134. DOMENICO CAMPAGNOLA

140. GIULIO CAMPI

143. AGOSTINO CARRACCI

144. AGOSTINO CARRACCI

162. ANNIBALE CARRACCI

165. ANNIBALE CARRACCI

173. LODOVICO CARRACCI

178. LODOVICO CARRACCI

198. LODOVICO CIGOLI

199. LODOVICO CIGOLI

200. ROMULO CINCINNATO

203. ANTONIO CORREGGIO

209. DANIELE DA VOLTERRA

211. DANIELE DA VOLTERRA

215. JACOPO DA EMPOLI

218. PIETRO FACCINI

225. PAOLO FARINATO

227. GAUDENZIO FERRARI

228. GAUDENZIO FERRARI

232. FRANCIABIGIO

233. BATTISTA FRANCO

240. LATTANZIO GAMBARA

243. BERNARDINO GATTI

248. ? GIULIO ROMANO

282. GIACOMO LIGOZZI

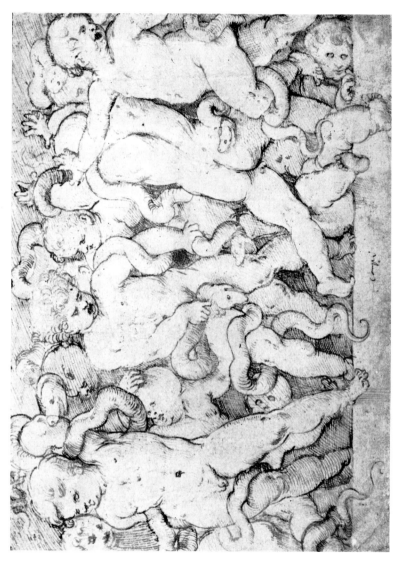

280. ALTOBELLO MELONI

291 *recto.* MICHELANGELO

291 *verso*. MICHELANGELO

293 *recto*.  MICHELANGELO

Micdel Angelo Bromarta

294. MICHELANGELO

296 *recto*. MICHELANGELO

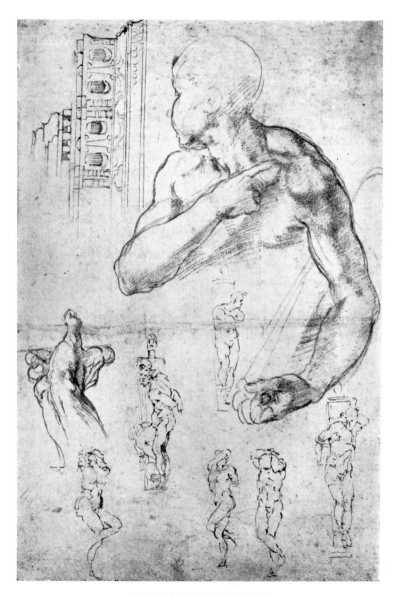

297 *recto*. MICHELANGELO

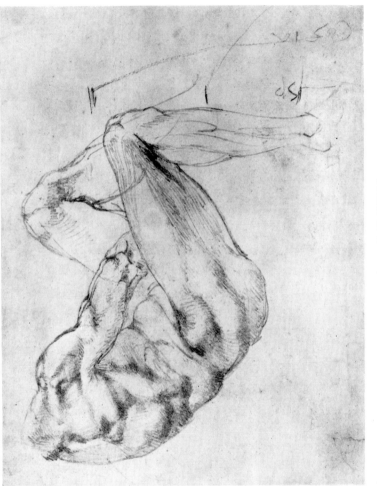

309 *recto.* MICHELANGELO

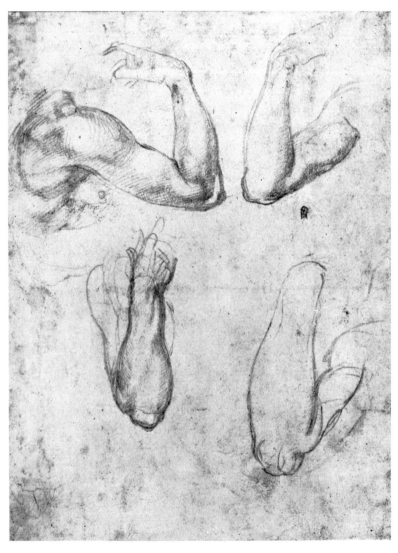

309 *verso*. MICHELANGELO

315. MICHELANGELO

316 *recto*. MICHELANGELO

316 *verso.* MICHELANGELO

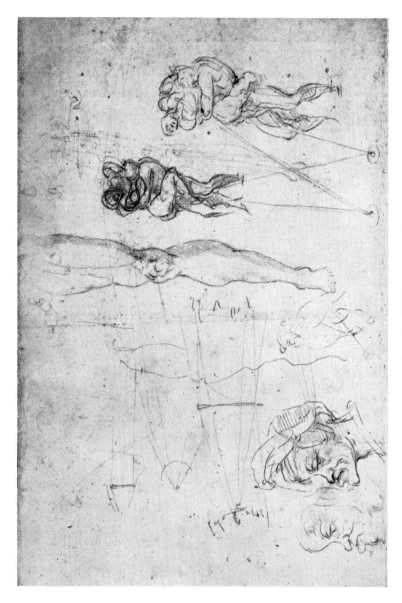

317 *recto*. MICHELANGELO

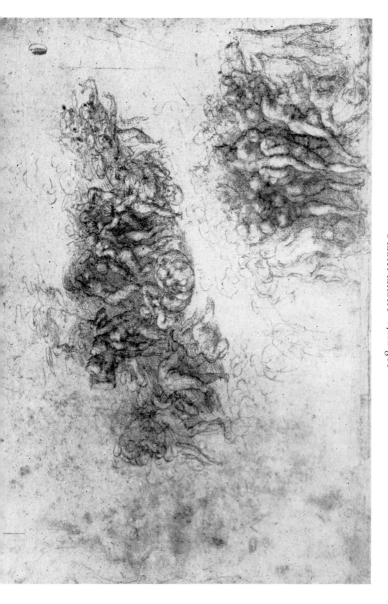

318 *recto*. MICHELANGELO

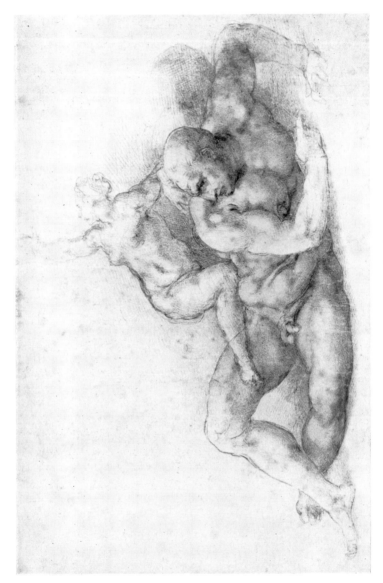

323 *recto.* MICHELANGELO

324. MICHELANGELO

325. MICHELANGELO

326. MICHELANGELO

327 *recto*. MICHELANGELO

330 *recto*. MICHELANGELO

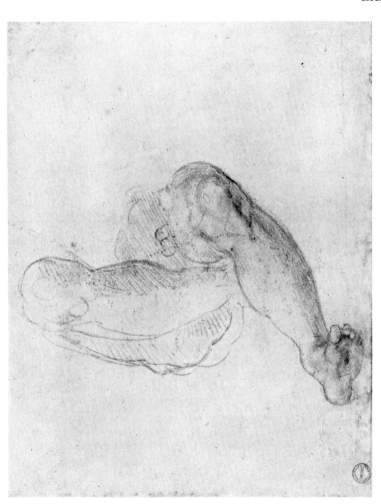

330 *verso.* MICHELANGELO

333 *recto*. MICHELANGELO

334 *recto*. MICHELANGELO

337 *recto*. MICHELANGELO

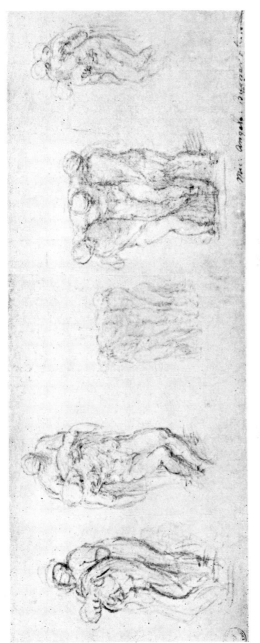

339. MICHELANGELO

342. MICHELANGELO

343 *recto*. MICHELANGELO

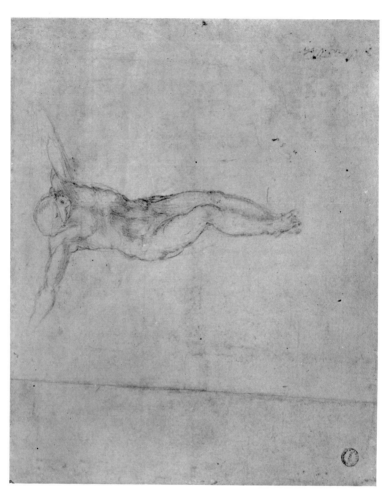

343 *verso.* MICHELANGELO

Messer francesco signior mio caro Grea alma bello di se
a fare e tai pare che col cardinale si sia facto noca figura
soza capo

344 *recto*. MICHELANGELO

345. MICHELANGELO

389. GIOVANNI BATTISTA MONTANO

420. LELIO ORSI

424. PALMA GIOVANE

425. PALMA GIOVANE

437. FRANCESCO PARMIGIANINO

440. FRANCESCO PARMIGIANINO

441. FRANCESCO PARMIGIANINO

442. FRANCESCO PARMIGIANINO

443. FRANCESCO PARMIGIANINO

452. BARTOLOMEO PASSAROTTI

454. BARTOLOMEO PASSAROTTI

460. BALDASSARE PERUZZI

464. BALDASSARE PERUZZI

471. BERNARDINO POCCETTI

472. BERNARDINO POCCETTI

490. GIOVANNI ANTONIO PORDENONE

491. ? ANDREA PREVITALI

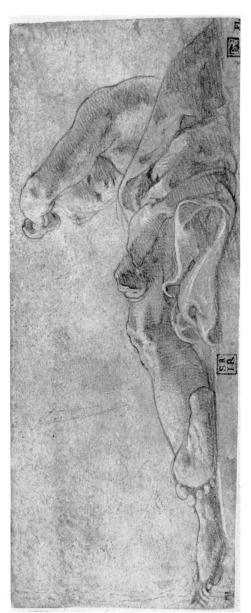

492. FRANCESCO PRIMATICCIO

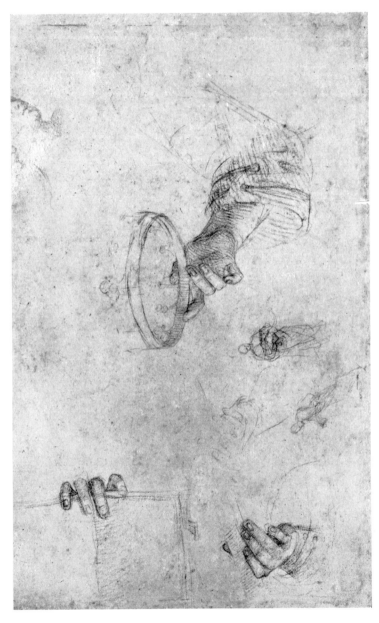

505. RAPHAEL

509. RAPHAEL

514 *recto*. RAPHAEL

515. RAPHAEL

517. RAPHAEL

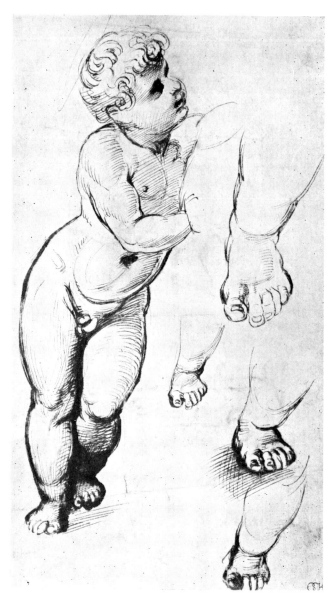

521. RAPHAEL

523. RAPHAEL

CXXIV

529. RAPHAEL

538 *recto*. RAPHAEL

539 *verso.* RAPHAEL

540. RAPHAEL

541 *recto*. RAPHAEL

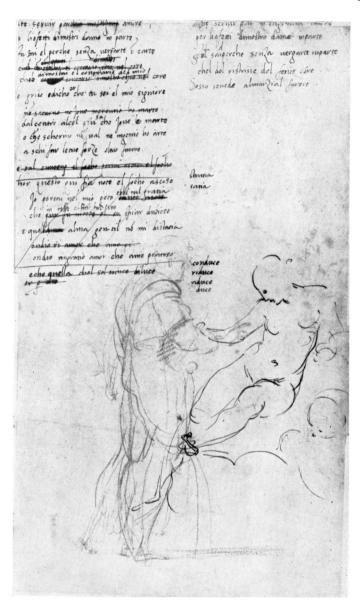

ite seguir ponsha — amore
e bespetti dimostri donne in parte
in sin el perche senza verterti e carte
— dimostr el compagnia del mio core
e grue edicho che tu sei el mio signore
ne sciuno ne one moreunir lo marte
dal centro alcel piu cho [que] lo morte
o che scherme ne val ne imemir bo arte
a sem for lerie force slow furore
e — el — el —
hor questo piu fra noto el focho ascoso
Jo governi nel mio poto — ebbi tal gratia
che — in — citir — ben —
e quell — alma gentil ne mi distancia
— si — che — one —
ondio ingrauir amor che ome picroso
eche quella chel sol vince viluce
or — —

per lesam dimostro danne inparte
si in superche senza vergouir inparte
chel dol ristrisse del ferire cove
desso senede almangial furore

stancia
caria

conduce
riduce
nduce
duce

545 *verso*. RAPHAEL

551. RAPHAEL

552. RAPHAEL

554 *recto*. RAPHAEL

556. RAPHAEL

557 *recto*. RAPHAEL

559 *recto*. RAPHAEL

561. RAPHAEL

562. RAPHAEL

563. RAPHAEL

564. RAPHAEL

565. RAPHAEL

566 *recto*. RAPHAEL

567. RAPHAEL

568. RAPHAEL

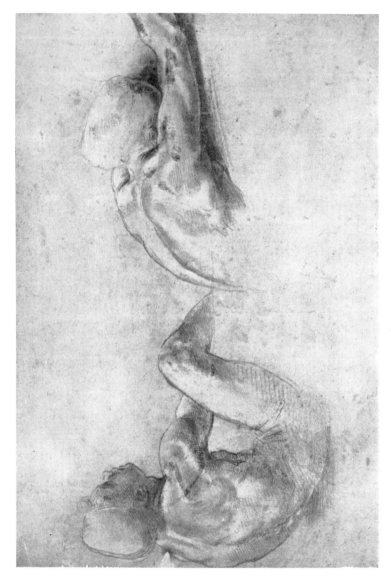

570. SCHOOL OF RAPHAEL

573. SCHOOL OF RAPHAEL

679. FRANCESCO SALVIATI

681. FRANCESCO SALVIATI

683. FRANCESCO SALVIATI

687. GUISEPPE SALVIATI

688. GIUSEPPE SALVIATI

692. ANDREA DEL SARTO

700. GIOVANNI ANTONIO SODOMA

793. VINCENZO TAMAGNI

716. JACOPO TINTORETTO

718. TITIAN

720. SANTI DI TITO

727. GIOVANNI DA UDINE

730. PERINO DEL VAGA

731. PERINO DEL VAGA

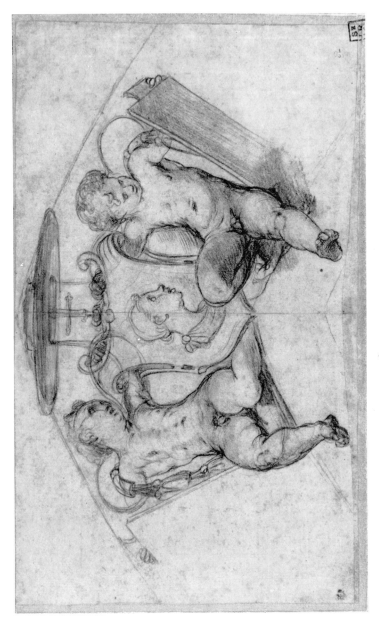

733. FRANCESCO VANNI

740. GIORGIO VASARI

744. PAOLO VERONESE

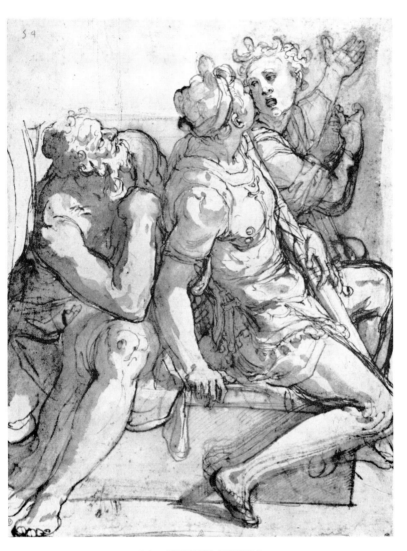

751. FEDERIGO ZUCCARO

752. FEDERIGO ZUCCARO

766. TADDEO ZUCCARO

765. TADDEO ZUCCARO

786. STEFANO DELLA BELLA

790. STEFANO DELLA BELLA

795. LORENZO BERNINI

792. LORENZO BERNINI

793. LORENZO BERNINI

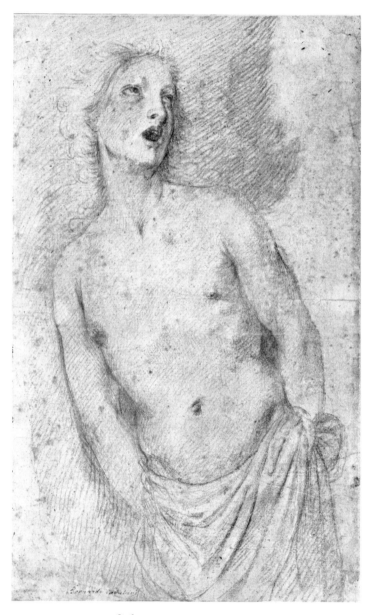

816. BERNARDO CAVALLINO

825. AGOSTINO CIAMPELLI

838. CARLO DOLCI

839. DOMENICHINO

842. DOMENICHINO

844. FERRAÙ FENZONI

851. FRANCESCO GRIMALDI

856. GUERCINO

863. GUERCINO

858. GUERCINO

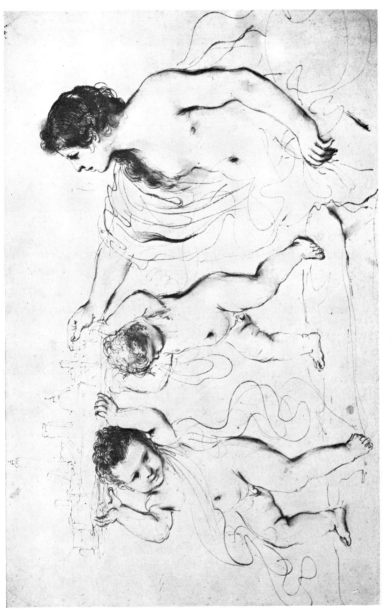

862. GUERCINO

861. GUERCINO

879. OTTAVIO LEONI

884. OTTAVIO LEONI

896. FRANCESCO MAFFEI

898. GIOVANNI MANNOZZI

900.  CARLO MARATTI

902. CARLO MARATTI

910. PIER FRANCESCO MOLA

914. PIER FRANCESCO MOLA

926. MATTIA PRETI

928. MATTIA PRETI

931. GUIDO RENI

932. GUIDO RENI

943. GIOVANNI BATTISTA SASSOFERRATO

955. FRANCESCO SOLIMENA

980. ANTONIO CANALETTO

976. ANTONIO CANALETTO

996. FRANCESCO FONTEBASSO

997. FRANCESCO FONTEBASSO

999. GAETANO GANDOLFI

1004. PIER LEONE GHEZZI

1005. ANTONIO GIONIMA

FRANCESCO GUARDI

1009.

1013. FRANCESCO GUARDI

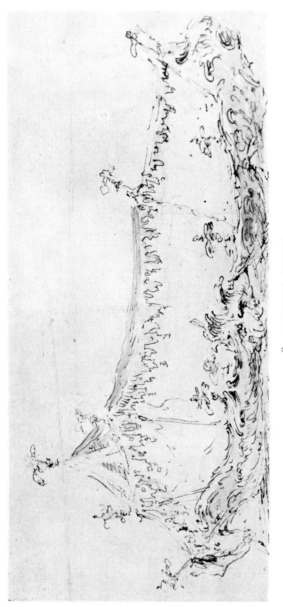

1018. FRANCESCO GUARDI

1014. FRANCESCO GUARDI

1015. FRANCESCO GUARDI

1023. ALESSANDRO MAGNASCO

1026. AGOSTINO MASUCCI

1031. GIOVANNI PAOLO PANNINI

1034. GIOVANNI BATTISTA PIAZZETTA

1035. GIOVANNI BATTISTA PIAZZETTA

1042. GIOVANNI BATTISTA PIRANESI

1038. GIOVANNI BATTISTA PIRANESI

1069. MARCO RICCI

1081. GIOVANNI BATTISTA TIEPOLO

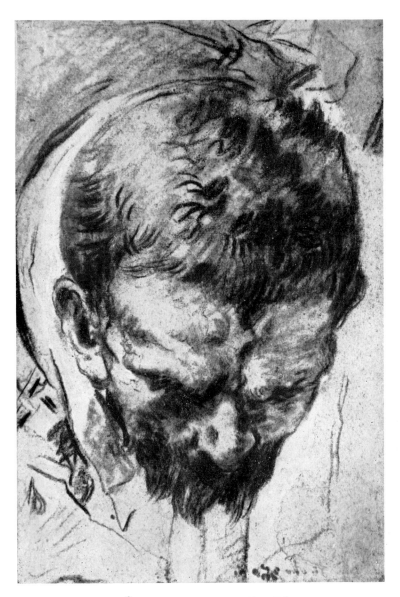

1080. GIOVANNI BATTISTA TIEPOLO

1077. GIOVANNI BATTISTA TIEPOLO

1082. GIOVANNI BATTISTA TIEPOLO

1087. DOMENICO TIEPOLO

1088. DOMENICO TIEPOLO

1098. DOMENICO TIEPOLO

1100. DOMENICO TIEPOLO

1112. BARTOLOMEO PINELLI